DANCING
FOR
JOY

DANCING FOR JOY

A Biblical Approach to Praise and Worship

MURRAY SILBERLING

LEDERER MESSIANIC PUBLISHERS
Baltimore, Maryland

©1995 by Murray Silberling. All rights reserved.
Published by Lederer Messianic Publishers
6204 Park Heights Avenue, Baltimore, MD 21215 U.S.A.
Call for a complete catalog of Messianic products—
books, videos, tapes, CDs, Judaica, and more.
(410) 358-6471
ISBN 1-880226-62-6
Printed in the United States of America
Cover & Book Design by Steffi Rubin

I want to thank my wife, Kay, who encouraged me when I felt like there were not enough hours in the day to write this book. She was always there to support and assist me. A special thank you to my children, Lonnie and Jordan, who gave up precious computer game time so that I could finish the book. In a family there is no such thing as a task that does not affect the entire family. Thank you.

Let them praise his name with dancing...
Psalm 149:3

FOREWORD

Several years ago, I had the privilege of watching Murray Silberling dance. In fact, he was leading a group of people in dance at a conference of the Messianic Jewish Alliance of America. I'd seen people dancing there before; they always looked like they were enjoying themselves. But watching Murray lead them convinced me that dance is truly a form of worship.

I approached him about writing a book on dance. His first reaction was that he was very busy leading his congregation. I understood that. That's a full time job and then some. But after some discussion, this spiritual leader of a large Messianic congregation took on the challenge and said he would somehow find the time. He knew the importance of explaining dance as worship.

We discussed what would make for the best book. Because worship dance is somewhat controversial among some of our brothers and sisters in the family of faith, Murray decided to first write a theology of dance as found in the Bible. After all, we didn't want to publish something without a solid theological basis. He has done an impressive job with this, examining the original Bible languages and coming up with some rather fascinating findings.

Tracing dance through Israel's past, as well as in the Church, this "dancing rabbi," as he is affectionately known in Messianic Jewish circles, lays an interesting foundation for modern worship through dance. He demonstrates how dance has been used through the ages as a way to facilitate the worship of God.

One especially encouraging aspect of *Dancing for Joy* is Murray's patient treatment of the dancing *klutz*. This is the person—generally a male—who feels too awkward to dance, or assumes that dancing is for women only. Even I, who do not dance, was encouraged to begin a dance ministry in my congregation, and even participate in it! Reading this part of Murray's book, I became convinced that I could experience a deeper, more worshipful time with the Lord by learning these dances. Same for my congregation.

We've included materials in the book from *Messianic Dance International*™, the ministry Murray has been involved with for many years. We're grateful to MDI for allowing us to adapt some of their materials for use here. If you're interested in learning how to do worship dance, you'll want to obtain their books, videos, and audio tapes. Contact Lederer Publishers and Distributors for these excellent resources.

Publishers don't often write forewords for their authors. Usually they get a famous person to commend the book. But I wanted to explain how this work came about. Most often, people send us manuscripts that we review and consider for publication. If we think there's a place for a particular book, we publish it.

In this case, we approached Murray Silberling to write *Dancing for Joy* because we knew, as a reputable theologian he would properly handle the theology of dance, as a respected pastor, he would deal with the ministry value of dance, and as a dancer, himself, he would help us learn just how to begin dancing for joy.

I know you'll enjoy and be challenged by reading this book.

BARRY RUBIN

Executive Director, Lederer Messianic Ministries
Publisher, Lederer Messianic Publishers

PREFACE

When I first became involved in Messianic dance nine years ago, they dubbed me "the dancing Rabbi." I am not called this because I am a great dancer. They saw dancing that did not have anything to do with skill, grace, or rhythm. It had to do with *joy*. I love to praise and worship my God with my whole "heart, soul, and might."

Over the years I have had many people come up to me to say how blessed and inspired they were to watch me dance. I have had many Messianic rabbis tell me that down deep they wish they could dance with such exultation.

At first, it seemed rather odd to me that others did not enjoy this wonderful form of manifesting God's love. I had caught a vision that all of the body of Messiah would be dancing together. I began to pray that the Lord would reveal to me how to help spread this vision for dance by showing me why others did not dance and how to overcome their reluctance.

Being one to take obstacles as opportunities, I began to develop a philosophy of Messianic dance that would make it easy to develop a Messianic dance ministry. Since then, this philosophy has spread that initial vision to Messianic synagogues and churches in every region of the country. An outgrowth of this philosophy was a project that I called *Messianic Dance International.*™ It included dance curriculum, audio tapes, and videos that help congregations get started in dance ministry. I have seen these materials work in many congregations throughout the world.

Whenever people catch that vision and begin dancing I know that great and powerful changes will soon be occurring in their lives. Just as Moses wished that all God's people would prophesy (Numbers 11:29), so I wish that all God's people could dance before Him.

I wrote this book to encourage Messianic synagogues and churches to begin their own congregational dance ministries. I want to assure leaders that Messianic dance is truly Biblical, historical, and revitalizing. I want to strengthen the heart of all those who have sensed that God is calling their congregation to express their worship in this form. I hope that this book will enable anyone who desires to dance, whether male, female, young, or old to catch the vision. I especially have a heart to see more people dancing. I truly expect that this book will be informational and inspirational. I know that it will be a good resource for anyone who desires involvement in dance ministry.

I believe that one day the entire body of Messiah will be dancing before his throne. Dance is the most powerful expression of intimacy between God and his children. My desire is that *you* begin to dance before the Lord, today!

TABLE OF CONTENTS

DANCING
FOR
JOY

1

BIBLICAL FOUNDATIONS OF DANCE

Religious revivals are often accompanied by the restoration of older forms of worship. These forms are modified to express the culture and consensus of the times. Today, there is a revival of dance within the Messianic Jewish movement. The use of dance in praise and worship has not only become a hallmark of the Messianic expression, but has significantly struck a chord in the heart of the Church as a whole.

The desire to infuse the Spirit of God into new forms of worship has sent the body of Messiah searching outside of conventional styles of worship. In this quest, many believers, both within and apart from the Messianic movement, have become involved with this new breath of the Spirit in dance.

Maybe you have experienced dance in a Messianic congregation and thought how wonderful it would be if your Messianic congregation or church could have dance as a part of its expression of worship. First you tried to picture the look on your rabbi's or pastor's face as several new enthusiasts got up to dance during one of your worship songs. There is the fear that some congregants would abuse or misuse this form of worship in order to do their own thing. The vivid thought of a chaotic service might paralyze you with fear. As you try to rid yourself of these horrendous thoughts, you hastily decide to forget the whole crazy idea.

I believe that this book will help you, your rabbi or pastor, and your congregation to begin to develop in the area of dance. The experience of many Messianic synagogues and churches has led to an overwhelming sense of revival and a fresh awareness of the Spirit of God in the midst of their congregation.

As you discover the biblical and historical roots of dance, I think that you will become less fearful about its use in your congregation. With some explanations of the forms, styles, and uses of dance, you will be more knowledgeable in the proper exercise of dance in worship. I expect that your efforts will stretch beyond your comfort zone. Sometimes that is exactly what we need to make new wineskins for revival in our lives and our congregations.

Traditionally, dance has been perceived by many believers as something to be feared. Many Messianic Jews have spent a good amount of time in a church, and have adopted a negative attitude towards dance. In addition, a wide range of Christian denominations relate to a pietistic tradition that perceived dance as the first step on a slippery slope toward sensual temptations.

All dancing, even sacred dance, has more or less been viewed over the last two hundred years as too much of a sexual temptation for the believer. This biased view gave support to those who used or misused the Bible in order to prove that dance was something for every believer to avoid. Dance was discouraged in any form. But when we are challenged to delve into the Scriptures to defend this bias, we find that the Bible gives us an altogether different perspective.

In the first few chapters of this book, you will discover a convincing portrait of dance in biblical theology, history, and culture. You will also find a strong scriptural foundation for my view of dance. In later sections, I will try to convey a practical vision and philosophy of dance, including how to establish a dance ministry within your congregation. You can personally begin to discover, develop, and grow in this very lively form of worship.

Before we get too involved in the numerous examples of dance in the Hebrew Scriptures and the New Covenant, we need to first look at several of the specific Hebrew words that are translated as dance. The principle word for dance in the Scriptures is the word *khul* (חול), which denotes a circling or ring dance. *Khul* is usually used in its various forms of *makhol* (מחול)and *mekholah* (מחולה).

Another word for dance is *raqad* (רקד), which literally means "to skip" or "leap." The Hebrew word *gil* (גיל) is often translated as rejoice, but literally means "to spin around in joy." This word has tremendous significance. Zephaniah 3:17 says, "The Lord your God in the midst of thee [is] mighty; he will save, he will rejoice over thee with joy; he will rest in his love, he will *joy* over thee with singing." The word that is translated "he will joy" is the term *yagil* (יגיל). The literal translation then would be that God dances with joy over us! Can you imagine God dancing over his people? If God can dance with joy, how much more should we dance with joy since he is in our midst?

In total, there are some thirteen words that are either directly translated as dance or translated rejoice, but denote dance as the actual form of rejoicing. Recent studies suggest that the words for "rejoice" and "dance" are the same words in Aramaic. Aramaic was the language most commonly spoken in Israel during the time of Yeshua (the Hebrew name for Jesus).

The extensive use of the word "rejoice" to denote dance in such a wide variety of words gives us a glimpse of the central use of dance within Hebrew culture. The young maidens of ancient Israel were pictured going up to Shiloh each year for "The Lord's feast", "to dance in dances" (לחול במחולות, *lakhul ba mekholot*) before the Lord (Judges 21:19–23). To proclaim God's goodness in the harvest was a common use of dance. Since there were many different harvest times in the year, dance was a regular illustration of the joy of harvest.

Scholars maintain that the Hebrew word *khag* (חג), commonly translated "festival," originally denoted the sacred circle dance performed around the altar in the sanctuary. This suggests that the essence and nature of festival and dance were so intertwined that when a Jewish person spoke of a festival their first thought would be of dancing in joyful celebration. In his book *Worship And Dance*, J.H. Eaton says, "In many Old Testament passages alluding to cultic rejoicing but without explicit mention of dancing we can safely assume that dancing is implied."[1] Even today, in the Hebrew language, the common greeting for any of the joyous holidays is *khag sameakh* (חג שמח) which might be translated, "a joyful festival."

There are numerous biblical examples of dance among the Israelites that proclaim victory during war. Whenever Israel won in battle, dance was a primary expression of their gratitude to the Lord. Victorious dance also declared to all the other nations that the Lord was the one true God. Later, we will look at dance used in spiritual warfare.

Another principal use of dance within the ancient Middle Eastern culture was to show hospitality. Families would join with their guests in dancing. Examples of this kind of hospitality appear in Judges 11:34 and Luke 15:25.

The biblical festivals of the Jewish calendar gave many opportunities to rejoice in dance. During the Feast of Booths (*Sukkot*), one of the oldest agricultural celebrations in biblical history, an annual torch dance was performed. This dance was conducted by the men of the community.

In addition to sacred dances for holy days, the life-cycles of Israel were special occasions to rejoice in dance. The birth of a child, circumcision, the *pidyon ha ben* or redemption of the firstborn, coming of age at twelve or thirteen (known today as the Bat or Bar Mitzvah), betrothal and marriage were all times to dance.

The life of Yeshua is a wonderful example of these celebrations. In Luke 2:21, 22, and 2:42, we find descriptions of his circumcision, pidyon ha ben, and coming of age. We can expect that many of these celebrations included dancing. Another example of a life-cycle celebration is the wedding at Cana (John 2:1). Even today, no Jewish wedding is complete without the traditional dances.

Both in the biblical and later Jewish traditions, dance was the primary manner of celebrating deliverance. In Exodus 15:20, the dance of the Israelites after their deliverance from Egypt expressed the joy of their freedom. This salvation event was a watershed occurrence in the history of Israel. It divides the mourning and bondage of past slavery from the future freedom of Israel to worship their God. The first act of community rejoicing was affirmed through the celebration of dance.

In the era of Samuel and the prophets, dance was an ecstatic expression of the intimate relationship between the Lord and his true prophets. On one occasion, Saul was caught up in the Spirit of prophesying, and "was changed into another man" (1 Samuel 10:5). The word used here for the prophetic "band" of men is the Hebrew word *khevel* (חבל), which can be translated as "cord" or "rope," and implies the practice of the circle dance. In verses 5–7, the prophets use dance in order to become vessels for the Word of the Lord, allowing themselves to be overcome by the Spirit of God so that the Lord might speak to the people through them. Dancing was a means for the prophets to ready themselves to receive the Spirit of the Lord, focusing their entire body, soul, and spirit on the Word of God. As with Saul, a dynamic transformation took place when these men danced before the Lord. The change was so dramatic in Saul's case that he was considered to have changed into an entirely different person.

King David is famous for leading the community of Israel in dancing and singing. In 2 Samuel 6:14, he danced before the Lord with all of his heart. His disregard for his royal position and demeanor brought chastening from his wife, Michal. We usually think of David dancing before the Lord as a chaotic leaping and skipping in wild abandon. On the contrary, the word used to describe his dancing refers to a choreographed dance that was characteristic of community joy in the presence of the Lord.

David also used communal dance to develop a consciousness of community among the people. Doug Adams, in *Congregational Dancing in Christian Worship*, suggests that "David's military success has been attributed to the troupes' coordination and esprit de corps attained through training and dance."[2]

Although David was known to dance after his numerous victories, his psalms reflect a variety of experiences that led him to dance before the Lord. In Psalm 30:2, David recounted an experience of forgiveness that grew into a desire to dance in joy. In Psalms 149:3 and 150:4, he commanded the people to praise the Lord in dance.

More than 600 years after David, the prophet Jeremiah described the tragic captivity of Israel and the exile to Babylon in his Lamentations. On their way to Babylon, the Israelites sang by the river Chebar, repenting for their sins and lack of trust in God (Psalm 137).

One of the most prominent signs of exile was the disruption of dance. In Lamentations 5:15, Jeremiah declares that a sign of Israel's spiritual poverty is the cessation of dance in their community. The sound of mourning replaced the joyful sounds of dance at festivals, weddings, and worship in the Temple which ended with its destruction.

Even before the devastation of the exile upon the Israelites, Jeremiah foretold the nation's restoration. Jeremiah 31:13 prophesies, "Then shall the virgin rejoice in the dance...and I will turn their mourning into joy." J.G. Davies characterizes this section of Scripture by saying, "the day was to come when a new covenant would be inaugurated. Here dance is given a future and an eschatological dimension..."[3] In other words, the prophets saw dance as one of the manifestations of the relationship between the Lord and his people. The future is depicted by a New Covenant, *B'rit Chadashah*, when Messiah will bring in the Messianic kingdom, *olam habah*. This renewal is characterized by the restoration to Israel of their symbol of joy—dance. What could be more appropriate than for Messianic Jewish and non-Jewish believers to demonstrate the presence of God in their lives through dance?

The New Covenant was largely written by Jews in a Jewish context, so we would expect to find a Jewish attitude towards dance. In Luke 6:23, we see that dance was understood by Yeshua's contemporaries as the customary and appropriate way to express their joy. In Aramaic, the use of the word dance is generally associated with the rejoicing of a wedding, a Sabbath or a holy day. The Greek word *choron* (χορον) is from the word *choros* and is translated here as "rejoice." This word suggests a circular dance in ancient literature and is the root of our words choreography and chorus. At the wedding in Cana, dancing would be the expected sign of joy. In Luke 15:25, a group dance (*choros*) accompanies the return of the prodigal son to his father.

The scriptural facts about dance paint a very different view than the one traditionally held by many churches. Although the evidence for a positive attitude toward dance is impressive, throughout history many Christians refused to examine the evidence because of traditional or personal fears.

After the biblical period, dance may have become associated with pagan and secular societies, but we must not lose sight of its long sacred, biblical history. For comparison, consider the example of circumcision, which has also had a history of both sacred and profane use. Other nations before Abraham used religious circumcision, but God decreed this to be the sign of his covenant for Abraham and his descendants. God trusts us to be able to use dance in proper ways to glorify him. If God is not afraid of dance, why are we afraid of it?

There are no prohibitions against dance in the Bible. God never denounced dance as a practice to resist or avoid. There are examples of dance taking place in a negative context, but in all of these instances it was being misused either as a form of worship towards other gods, or in drunken orgies. We all agree with the need to stay away from these forms of worship.

The example found in Exodus 32:19, where the Israelites dance around the golden calf when Moses was up on Mount Sinai, is often referred to by those who oppose dance as worship. But it was not the dancing that angered Moses; it was the worship of the golden calf. Another commonly cited Scripture is the instance of some Pharisees who opposed Yeshua. Luke 7:32 suggests that they reprimanded Yeshua as one who refused to dance for them. Yeshua does not respond to these opponents. Some interpreters suggest that Yeshua's lack of a rejoinder is a model for his followers concerning dance. In fact, the type of dance indicated by the passage was a common form of rejoicing by the people. Yeshua's lack of response tells us that he will not be manipulated by others. This was not a universal condemnation of dance by Yeshua, but a repudiation of those who were trying to exploit him.

Another weak argument is the infamous dance of Herodias' daughter. This has been applied as a biblical blueprint for God's view on dance, although it is more a highlight on the misuse of dance. Furthermore, this example of an immoral use of dance took place during a period when dance was widely used in Israel for sacred purposes.

Israel associated dance with the exclusive worship and praise of the Lord, which was distinctly different than the Canaanite practice of dance, which used self-flagellation in order to placate and manipulate Baal. In 1 Kings 18:26, the prophets of Baal danced about the altar in futile attempts to manipulate their gods.

I believe that we are mature enough and can trust the Holy Spirit sufficiently to discern the difference between the manipulation of other gods and the worship of the one true God. Throughout history, there has been a tension that divides those who were willing to experiment in new forms of worship and those who were not. But the fact is, negative attitudes toward godly dance are hard to find in Scripture.

The biblical evidence reveals that dance was an integral part of Israel's worship throughout history. From the first pages of the Bible we find positive examples of dance. If we investigate the Scriptures, we will overcome any objections that prevent dance from serving as both a personal and congregational expression of our faith and joy. We stand on a firm foundation with respect to the place of dance in biblical worship.

Even with a strong biblical basis for the use of sacred dance, historically we will see that there have always been those who were afraid to use the gift of dance. In every area of congregational life we find those who do not have the spiritual discernment and maturity to separate the sacred from the profane. Rather than allow fear to keep us from God's good gifts, we must learn to use them appropriately.

Now that we have demonstrated the biblical foundations for dance as a form of worship, praise, and rejoicing, we can begin to develop a biblical philosophy of dance that is befitting our contemporary congregations and ministries. The continuity of dance throughout the Bible leads us to explore dance today as a form of praise and worship that the Holy Spirit is restoring to the body of Messiah.

The Messianic movement is in the forefront of this restoration of dance, but it is not for Messianic believers only. Many Christian congregations are using the knowledge, experiences, and resources of Messianic congregations to develop dance within their own congregations. Later, we will cover the practical aspects of getting dance started in a congregation, but first we need to learn from the mistakes of others. We also need to investigate the historical background of dance after the biblical period so that we do not make some of the same mistakes that have been made in the past.

2

HISTORICAL BACKGROUND
OF SACRED DANCE

Sacred dance is widely acknowledged as an important historical dimension of ancient biblical worship. But today, dance does not have any role in the worship services of the traditional synagogue and church. Since dance has become non-essential to our worship, both in the synagogue and church, we need to go back in history to see how it got this way. Did sacred dance continue in the synagogues beyond 70 C.E. (see note below) when the Temple was destroyed? How did the church react to this Jewish expression of worship? Did the church always resist finding a place for dance in worship and liturgy?

Communal dance in worship began with the earliest celebrations of Israel's existence as a nation, at the deliverance from Egypt. During the entire history of Jewish worship until the early Mishnaic period (2nd–3rd centuries C.E.) the people of God celebrated before him in dance. "A vision of heaven throughout the Talmud and Midrash includes the communal dance."[1]

Sadly, the use of dance as a religious practice declined with

---

Common Era is the period since the Messiah has come, often indicated by A.D. The term B.C.E.. refers to the period before the Common Era, before Yeshua.

the destruction of the Second Temple and the end of Sanhedrin authority in 70 C.E. Following the disastrous *Bar Kochba* rebellion against the Romans, around 132 C.E., sacred dance in Judaism virtually ceased. The significant reason for the decline was the Jewish trauma at being powerless and finally exiled from Jerusalem. After the destruction of the Temple and defeat at the hands of the Romans, Judaism saw itself again as the object of disapproval and judgment by God.

Again, as in the earlier exile to Babylon, the sounds of joy, mirth, song, and dance were abandoned. Sacred religious dance within the Jewish community did not return until the 1700's. The celebrations during *Simchat Torah* (Joy of Torah), at the end of the feast of *Sukkot* (Tabernacles), were an exception. The traditional dancing with the Torah scrolls has continued to this day.

Yet, as a secular folk or cultural expression of communal joy and Jewish life-cycle celebrations, dance has continued throughout history within the Jewish community. Weddings and *Bar* and *Bat Mitzvahs* are examples of these types of life-cycle observances where dancing is an integral part of Jewish life today.

The first signs of the popular renewal of sacred dance, beginning in the 18th century, lead us back to the scattered remnant of the Jewish people in Eastern Europe. In Judaism, sacred dance had virtually been suppressed after the Bar Kochba rebellion. But during the early 1700's a revivalist movement in Judaism sprang up in Poland called *Hasidism*. A defining characteristic of this movement was the expression of joy and intimacy with God through ecstatic dance. This movement quickly spread throughout the region, revolutionizing the Jewish community.

The founder of this movement was called the *Baal Shem Tov* (Master of the Good Name). Hasidism reintroduced joy, *simcha*, into the religious service. The Baal Shem Tov recaptured the use of dance to experience an intimate relationship with God. He taught that the dynamic of dance would fill a person with the joy of the Lord. Renowned for his stories, he recounted how he learned to dance in order to aid a jailed Jewish friend to gain his freedom. He claimed that if one could dance well, he or she would be freed from bondage.

Dancing is still a central part of worship in Hasidic circles. At the Western Wall in Jerusalem, as Friday evening draws near, you can see the exhilarating sight of orthodox Jewish students streaming out of their schools to welcome *Shabbat,* the Sabbath, with dance. Hasidism was the impetus for dance to slowly move back into other orthodox Jewish sects.

Philosophically, the Jewish people always connected sacred dance to their identity as God's chosen people. Dance continued in Jewish imagination as a primary expression of the Messianic age—when Israel would be restored as the head of the nations and peace would rule on earth.

We will now see how Christianity dealt with sacred dance. Most people assume that dance has not been a tradition of mainstream Christianity. They surmise that it must have ceased after the church's final separation from its Jewish roots, around the 3rd or 4th century. However, this is not the case. Dance was an essential part of Christian worship and liturgy up until the 1700's.

Dance was a part of the worship of the first followers of Yeshua and withstood the radical changes that transformed the early Messianic communities. These early believers, Jews who believed in Yeshua as the Jewish Messiah, had retained their Jewish lifestyle as the cultural framework for their faith. It was not until the late second and early third centuries with a preponderance of gentiles in leadership roles within the church that more radical changes occurred. Originally the question facing the believers had to do with whether the gentiles could be included in the community of believers, and if so, how (Acts 15). As early as 160 C.E., the issue was reversed, and the question became whether Jews were now excluded from the community of faith.

The primary ancient source of Christian liturgy and worship was the Temple service and later the synagogue service, in particular, the services of the Messianic synagogues. We often fail to appreciate how the early Messianic believers maintained their attachment to the Temple. The book of Acts repeatedly reminds us that the Temple was central for the community life and worship of Yeshua's first followers (Acts 2:46; 5:42; 21:27).

Two significant factors affected the use of dance in the development of the early Messianic synagogue service. The first was the destruction of the Temple in 70 C.E., which permanently altered the worship practices of the community. The problem was practical—lack of space.

The Messianic believers met in small synagogues and private homes. The loss of the Temple and its spacious courtyards meant that there were no ample places available for sacred dance. In their small synagogues and house meetings, space was at a premium. Dance, therefore, became a persistent, practical problem as the number of believers grew.

The second factor affecting the use of dance among early believers was the tendency to spiritualize elements of Jewish tradition. The early Messianic community in Jerusalem was Torah observant. Acts 21:20 reads, "Thou seest, brother, how many thousands of Jews there are which believe; and they are all zealous of the law." But over the next two centuries, the Messianic Jewish world went through some radical changes in cultural expression. Although all the early believers until around 45 C.E. were Jewish or converts to Judaism, the large numbers of gentiles coming into the faith brought with them crucial differences in cultural expression and identity.

Change within the Messianic community intensified in the 2nd century, after the Bar Kochba rebellion. In the ultimate act of Roman anti-Semitic fervor, Jews were banned from living in Jerusalem and massive deportations displaced the Jewish populace. One of the results was that the new leadership of the Messianic community in Jerusalem became fully gentile. The far reaching changes they brought in separated the body of believers from their Jewish roots and led to a process of de-Judaization.

History records the problems that the new gentile leaders had in weaning the remaining Messianic believers away from the

synagogue. Gentile leaders found it difficult to claim equal authority with their Jewish counterparts in matters concerning the Jewish
Scriptures, since few of them were fluent in Hebrew. These non-
Jewish leaders, who had very little understanding of the Jewish
traditions, found it increasingly difficult to hold authority over
their community. Many people, including some gentiles, were
looking to Judaism for their foundational beliefs and life-cycle
practices. Because the new leaders were unfamiliar with traditional
Judaism and Hebrew, they reinterpreted the Bible in their own
context and established new practices and theologies.

Following such teachers as Origen, Justin Martyr, John
Chrysostom, the historian Eusebius, and the famous theologian,
Augustine, church theology changed to reflect the leaders' Hellenistic culture. Church theology reinterpreted itself in line with their
Neo-Platonic philosophy, and a mounting tension developed with
anything that was Jewish. Allegorical interpretation of the Scriptures was a tool that enabled the church leaders to spiritualize
elements of Jewish teaching and tradition. This set up a paradox in
Christian theological development. While the church attempted to
remain true to its biblical roots, which were Jewish, it was trying to
separate itself from the culture, authority, and beliefs of the Jews.

Although one might suspect that the de-Judaized church
would have succeeded in eliminating dance completely from the
worship service, that is not the case. The church underwent a
cultural transitional process over an extended period of time that
affected every aspect of belief and behavior. One can see the hand
of the Holy Spirit protecting dance during this precarious period of
change within the church.

In spite of the de-Judaization process, sacred dance continued to flourish within the church. From the time of the first
Messianic community, dance was described as an experience of
heavenly joy, an act of encountering and adoring the divinity of
God. Both the Messianic believers and the divine angels in heaven
were depicted in adoration of Yeshua through dance. Two of the
earliest liturgies record in detail the use of dance within the service.

Justin Martyr (100–165 C.E.) and Hippolytus (200 C.E.) both describe joyful circle dances as a part of the order of worship.

By applying the Platonic concept that things on earth are a reflection of the true pattern that is in heaven, the Hellenized theology of the church integrated the Jewish traditions of sacred dance. The scriptural tradition of dancing in heaven gave sanction for the church to use dance in liturgical worship. In the famous Shepherd of Hermes, as early as the first third of the second century, dance was perceived as part of the celestial bliss.[2] Clement of Alexandria (150–216 C.E.) in his *Address to the Heathens*, says, "When persons dance on earth, they also dance with the angels."[3] The idea of dance as spiritual worship copying heavenly worship is further established by an apocryphal text from the second century C.E., in which Yeshua is depicted as the leader of the dance.

In the apocryphal *Acts of John*, there is a long hymn called the "Hymn of Christ," where the ritual calls for the people to respond by circling the dancing figure of Yeshua. He commands his followers, "Answer to my dancing. See thyself in Me who speak and dancing what I do..." This hymn goes on to speak about dance. "To the universe belongs the dancer—Amen. He who does not dance does not know what happens—Amen."[4] This hymn is describing a spiritualized dance that enables the dancer to know God better.

With the political-ecclesiastical alliance forged by the influencial church historian, Eusebius Pamphilius, and the Emperor Constantine (306–337 C.E.), the role and significance of Jewish culture was greatly diminished. After this time, the Jewish people lost the rights of full citizens in the Roman Empire. No longer was the Jewishness of dance an issue.

Despite the transformation in church culture, the early Church Fathers supported the use of dance as prayer and worship in various forms. While some tried to spiritualize or eliminate dance from worship, many Church Fathers expressed that dance was an important part of the believer's relationship with God. John Chrysostom and Augustine were in agreement that dance brought one's bodily members into accord with the love of God.

Some early leaders, like Epiphanius (315–403 C.E.), sought to spiritualize dance. Like others he used the allegorical method of teaching Scripture, in which the physical aspects of the kingdom were primarily interpreted as representing spiritual or heavenly reality. Epiphanius taught that dance was to consist of symbolic movements of the soul, rather than actual physical movements, thereby giving credence to dance, without allowing it to be performed.

Dance was incorporated in the church, yet controlled by transforming it into liturgical processions and elaborately choreographed eucharistic celebrations. An example of the official place of dance and processions in the church is the Eastern priestly installation rites. The church established a ritual practice in which a new priest would circle the altar with his congregants as a part of his installation. This was a way to show the equality of the priest with his congregation and knit them together as a body. This practice persists today in the Orthodox Church.

Tensions developed within the church due to a desire for dance to enhance sacred worship on one hand, and the fear of abuse by newly converted pagans on the other. Dance was widely popular in pagan celebrations and rituals. When they became believers, sometimes their sensuous pagan dances came with them into the new faith. Bizarre dance practices within graveyards are recorded that revolved around the "dance for the dead." You can imagine how macabre and occult-like some of these dances might have been. Nevertheless, the new converts were encouraged to convert the dances from their pagan roots.

Throughout church history the official assaults on dance continued, along with efforts to free dance for proper use as an official expression of worship. There has not been a period when there was not some form of dance associated with the practice of Catholicism. Over the years, the church tried to allow dance into worship while keeping it in check through various council decrees. Their attempts were made, not in order to squelch dance altogether, but to ameliorate the abuses. For the first seventeen centuries, dance was an integral part of the church service in one form or another.

According to Louis Backman, a noted historian of dance, the Reformation, beginning in 1525, single-handedly brought about an almost total demise of dance within the Protestant churches. There are two major reasons behind the cessation of dance.

Unusual as it may seem, the first reason for the curtailment of dance over the next century and a half was the invention of the printing press. Along with fostering the spread of critical attitudes toward traditional church customs, the invention of the printing press had a considerable effect on all the arts. The printing press multiplied the publication of an enormous variety of tracts, pamphlets and books which were quickly and cheaply published. In 1545, the Council of Trent was convened to deal with the resulting religious confusion felt by the people. The decisions by this council sounded the eventual death-knell for liturgical dance, for processions, and for most visual arts within the church. Only the arts of printing, preaching, and music survived intact after the Reformation.

Martin Luther (1483–1546), the leading voice of the Reformation, had a very negative attitude towards dance. He saw no reason for dance within the service of the church. The effect of the Council of Trent and Martin Luther's influence prevented even dancing by the clergy and all dance was virtually suppressed by the late 1700's. Still, even with this suppression, one can see small glimmers today of the earlier traditions.

The second reason for the cessation of dance in Protestantism was the entrance of rationalism with its more critical view of the arts. This philosophy held the notion that the mind had priority over the body. During this time, there was a resumption of the de-Judaized, Hellenistic, mind-body dualism that had hindered the use of dance in the early years of the Church. The theology of the period stressed the rational over the experiential. Dance was determined to be too subjective to be appropriate for church liturgy.

For all intents and purposes, dance is barely recognizable today in Christianity. Sacred dance is submerged in the various liturgical movements of the body by the clergy. Token movements such as raised arms, upturned palms in the benediction, bowed head, kneeling and genuflecting, are all that remain of the richness of dance within the church. Dance processionals, eucharistic and festival dances, became a shadow of former practices. Eventually many of the movements that were a part of liturgical dance by the congregation were assumed by the clergy.

Wthin the Roman Catholic church, the Mass itself came to be perceived as the only appropriate form of dance. The minimal body movements by the priests during the Mass along with the limited movements of the congregants were the sum total of what was left of its rich Hebraic dance heritage.

DANCE IN AMERICA

By the end of the eighteenth century, the practice of religious dance in the new world was scarce and scattered. In 1774, a unique sect with Puritan roots, called "Shakers," came to America from England. The Shakers are one of the few denominations who stand apart from an almost total ban on dance within the American churches. Like many of the Puritans, they found their spiritual roots in the ancient biblical traditions that preceded church tradition. Their theology was unique from many of the other reformation groups due to an impassioned and clear understanding of their biblically based debt to the Jews.

They also had a profound sense of the prophetic future for the conversion of the Jewish people, largely based on Paul's writings in Romans chapter 11. Robert Leighton of Newbattle, Scotland, preached that, "Christ came of the Jews, and came first to them....Undoubtedly, that people of the Jews shall once more be commanded to arise and shine, and their return shall be the riches of the Gentiles."[5]

The Shakers created intricately choreographed dances. The men and women would move in separate groups with several shuffling steps forward and several back. These groups would advance and retreat while they would shake. They shook their hands with palms up and then down. Palms up signified the receiving of the Holy Spirit, while palms down represented the shaking off of sin.

The Shaker movement by and large came to an end in the late nineteenth century due to a self-imposed ruling against marriage. The decree to cease propagating led to their rapid decline. Nevertheless, small groups of Shakers persist in the United States to this day.

Another exception to the virtual cessation of contemporary dance within the church has been a recent revival of dance in the Green Mountains of Vermont. The Benedictine Monks of Weston Priory in Vermont have rediscovered sacred dance and are attempting to restore dance to its proper place within their community. Founded by Brother Leo in 1953, these Christians worship in joyful communal dance. Brother Leo was formerly the Abbot of Dormition Abbey in Jerusalem. There he discovered the rich Jewish roots of his faith, which he found included dance.

An interesting pattern has emerged in the last few centuries. As various sects of the church have regained their historical and theological roots in the Jewish people, sacred dance has reappeared as a form of religious worship. Whenever the Christian church has rid itself of its anti-Jewish attitudes and restored an appreciation for an experiential, rather than a merely rational faith, it is able to rediscover dance as a fruitful form of biblical worship. It is not surprising that the greater the attachment of the church to its Jewish roots, the richer its biblical faith. The metaphor of the olive tree in Romans chapter eleven illustrates that when the church draws on its roots it receives the rich nourishment of its heritage.

Over the last ten or fifteen years, the Christian church especially among the liturgical churches, has made large strides toward a proper use of sacred dance. Dance is now being performed in many churches. Most of this is modern dance, consisting of interpretive performance dances, which will be addressed in a later chapter.

MESSIANIC DANCE

Over the last twenty years, the Messianic movement has developed an authentic biblical and historic form of communal worship dance that is practiced by the entire community, young, old, men, women, and clergy. The present-day Messianic movement finds its forebears in the first-century Jews who believed the message that Yeshua is the Messiah.

The Jesus movement of the late 1960's included a large number of Jews coming to faith in Messiah. These young people attached themselves to older Jewish believers, who called themselves Hebrew-Christians. Some of these older believers had established congregational ministries, but many were involved in traditional churches or mission societies.

In 1967, during the dramatic Six-Day War, Jerusalem became once again a Jewish city, the capital of the Jewish state. A few years later, Israel was again fighting for survival during the 1973 Yom Kippur War. Inspired by world events, the new generation of Jewish believers were determined to get back to their roots. They insisted on expressing their Jewish identity in worship and adopted the title "Messianic Jews" in order to maintain their links with their families and the Jewish community.

Since 1968, the present day Messianic movement has flourished, beginning with several Messianic congregations in various parts of the country. In just twenty-five short years, the movement has grown to include congregations all over the world, including over 150 congregations in the United States alone. The Messianic Jewish movement identified strongly with the prophetic biblical promises to Israel and with modern Israelis whose culture is steeped in dance.

A major component of the Messianic revival involves the restoration of sacred dance. Sometimes called Messianic or Davidic worship, the Messianic movement has led the way in the choreography, teaching and development of various forms of dance. They incorporated many elements of traditonal Hasidic dance, as well as Israeli and Yemenite folk dances. The acceptance of dance based on its biblical and Jewish roots has led to the restoration of ancient forms of praise and worship within the whole body of believers.

One of the earliest congregations to develop sacred dance was Beth Yeshua Congregation in Philadelphia. From Beth Yeshua, many other congregations began experimenting with Israeli and Messianic dance in congregational worship. Today, almost every Messianic congregation includes some dance as a part of their services. Many Messianic congregations have dance classes or workshops that are open to their communities. In the last few years more and more representatives from the church have come to Messianic congregations to learn how to develop dance in their own churches. At the end of this book we will talk more about how to get a dance ministry started and provide further resource information.

3

PHILOSOPHY OF
CONGREGATIONAL DANCE

There are many forms and styles of dance that can be used to build up a congregation and bless the Lord. In the present Messianic movement there is a revival of dance that is founded on and continuous with biblical and historical sacred dance. The rapid growth of dance in the movement is due to a vision and philosophy of dance as an integral part of congregational life for anyone who desires to worship in this manner, and not just a few skilled dancers. My vision has always been to make it possible for the greatest number of people to praise and worship in dance and be able to do so in their own congregations.

We often see dance as a special performance for a specific occasion. The occasion may be a Jewish wedding, Bar Mitzvah, or a congregational holiday performance for Passover or Resurrection Day. These are all wonderful opportunities for dance to bless the congregation. But for these opportunities to transform a community it is crucial that not only those who are gifted in dance be uplifted. Almost any member of the congregation should be able to participate in the dance. There is a powerful release of the Spirit

Joyous dancing at an outdoor wedding reception.

of God when a community harmonizes together in praise and worship.

These are the key elements that make this philosophy effective: keep the steps simple, use interchangeable dances for beginners, allow simple movements with flexibility in gender specific dance styles, and make special arrangements for young children. With these principles at work, your congregation can experience a fresh spiritual revival through dance.

SIMPLE STEPS

The first element that makes this goal attainable is keeping the dance steps simple. The Israeli dance step vocabulary is simple and easy to learn. Like any language, the steps build upon themselves as the dancer becomes more familiar with them and develops greater skill. In this way, the basic style of dance can be built upon by those who are skillful and able to develop more complex and increasingly difficult styles of their own. Even the most ungraceful person can learn some basic steps and join with the entire congregation in dance during the worship service.

In one of our congregations, we had a dancer who had a very

low-key and laid back style of dancing. There were no excessive movements of any kind in his manner. His feet stayed close to the ground and he lacked exaggerated arm or hand movements or big leaps. One night, this man had an opportunity to teach our beginners' class. I thought that he would not make a good teacher because of his reserved style, and assumed that students preferred instructors with more flamboyance. He not only loved teaching the class, but the students thought he was the best teacher they had ever had.

Beginners reported that his low-key manner made it easy for them to learn the basic steps. Later they could embellish it with their own unique style. While his dancing was not flamboyant, it was solid and easy to follow. You do not have to be a dance virtuoso to bless and minister to others in dance.

With this philosophy, even at the beginners level, you can learn enough of the basic dances to immediately participate fully in the praise and worship. Age is not a factor in learning to dance either, since even the elderly people in the congregation can enjoy congregational dancing. There was a couple in their early 90's in our congregation who loved to dance. Because the dances could be danced at either a simple, low-impact level or with more exuberance and intricacy, they were able to join in many of the dances.

Anyone can learn to worship in dance. You might think that you are an exception to the rule and that nobody can teach you to dance with grace or rhythm. You will be surprised! I learned my lesson a few years ago. There was a man in our congregation whom I considered too clumsy to dance. I did not think he would learn more than one or two easy dances before he got frustrated and quit. But he had determination and stuck to it. Within six months, to my amazement, he had learned enough of the dances to become a teacher for some of the beginning classes. His steps, too, were simple and easy to follow for the beginners, because he knew firsthand how to start simply and build upon what he had learned. He has choreographed a dance that is used today in many Messianic congregations.

In the last chapter, I referred to the Benedictine Monks of Weston Priory in the Green Mountains of Vermont. They have been worshipping in joyful circle dances for many years and, as I recently discovered, their success in getting full congregational involvement has been possible because they have a philosophy in practice that is very similar to ours. The monks dance both Israeli folk dances and their own choreographed worship dances using the simple Israeli steps as their foundation. They, too, have the philosophy of keeping the dances simple enough so everyone can take part. They are able to involve most of their congregation in sacred dance because of a desire and philosophy to make dance a normative form of worship, like singing.

INTERCHANGEABLE DANCE

A key element of our congregational dance philosophy is to use interchangeable dance. This allows more people to participate in worship dance within a relatively short time. An interchangeable dance is one that can be used for two or more songs. With so many different dances, you might assume that it would take forever to learn to participate fully. Interchangeable dances allow the beginner to learn a half dozen dances at first and join half the dances in a worship service. Since many songs are written in 4/4 time with choruses or verses typically lasting eight measures, a dance for one song can also be substituted for several others, as long as it meets the criteria of time and theme. Even someone who has been dancing for only a few weeks will be excited to dance several times during a worship service.

GENDER SPECIFIC MOVEMENTS

Many congregations have quite a few women dancers but very few men. I am always frustrated when I visit Messianic synagogues and see so many women enjoying worship in dance while the men stand by and watch. Often, men come up to me and say things like, "I wish I could dance like you." I tell them that they can.

I have come to realize that it is much more difficult to make

Men doing a circle dance

men feel comfortable in dance worship than women. The key is to make men feel more comfortable being themselves. When they see an agile dancer, be it male or female, they are intimidated because they do not perceive themselves as graceful enough to dance.

Our philosophy of dance enables men to gain easy access to dance worship—despite the common perception that dance is for women to express themselves in worship, not men. All that is necessary to change this view, both for men and women, is to make some the movements gender specific. For example, when women dance, they use their arms in very graceful movements that are uncomfortable for most men to perform. When women do a *hora* step with hands waving over their heads, most men feel uncomfortable with this hand movement. We changed the men's step so that they put their hands loosely by their sides while the women wave their hands.

In our Messianic dance training we have eliminated the more flamboyant hand and arm movements from the beginners' dances. The dance classes teach a basic style that is simple and comfortable for both men and women. These few, slight changes in the arm or hand movements can make men feel much more comfortable. As a result, our dance classes usually include as many men learning dances as women, if not more. When choreographing a new dance, I suggest that a couple of the male dancers review it first. They will indicate if there are some parts they find uncomfortable.

I have discovered that there is a special joy and strength that accompanies a large group of men dancing a variety of steps besides a simple *hora*. In our holiday dances, we always perform a special men's dance. These dances generate great excitement, both among the men performing the dances and among the congregational members.

Involving Children in Dance

Another group that is often either left out or sent to a corner during the dance is the children. In our congregation, we only allow those children who are eight years old or over to dance in a circle. When a large number of children join in the dance, we have a dance teacher form a concentric circle in the center to protect both the children and the adults and to assist the children to dance. At each service there is a teacher assigned to make a children's circle in the middle. The children feel much more secure and accepted as a part of the dance ministry, without the pressure of being a part of the adult circle.

Children can be more capable than adults of understanding the power of movement and embracing dance in worship. If we give them a safe and protected place to dance, we will find a whole new generation of dance instructors developing before our very eyes. I feel real *naches* (a Yiddish word expressing a parent's pride in their children) when I watch the children perform their first holiday dance performances.

To review, the key elements for creating a congregational vision for dance worship include simple steps and movements, interchangeable dances, gender specific movements and something special for the children. Each of these elements help make it possible, in a very practical way, to allow everyone in the congregation to be blessed by dance ministry.

Children participating in worship dance

When a third of the congregation gets up to worship in dance something dynamic happens. As more and more people catch the vision for congregational dance ministry within the body of Messiah, a fresh anointing of the Spirit of God will pour out a blessing upon his people.

Everyone desires their congregation to be a place where the Spirit of God resides in such a way as to draw us closer to him. We all want to be changed by the transforming power of God in our praise and worship. The Messianic movement is leading the body of Messiah into a mighty refreshing of the Lord through the restoration of this vital part of our biblical, Jewish heritage.

4

DANCE AS PRAISE AND WORSHIP

DANCE AS PRAISE

Praise dance is a declaration, proclamation and celebration of the love of God. Many of the traditional forms of sacred dance for biblical holidays, life-cycle celebrations and rituals are for praise. This style of dance reaches beyond time and space to communicate the inner strength of God's people.

First of all, the style of praise dance is declarative in nature. We declare the deep joy that is the foundation of our relationship with God. Psalm 22:3 says, "God inhabits the praises of his people." Our bodies become the manifestation of joy in the face of all our adversaries. There is a declaration of victory.

Proclamation is the witness and testimony of the dancers to everyone who is watching. We proclaim through our dance before all people and the hosts of heaven that Yeshua is our Messiah. God is revealed to all the nations through our dance affirmations. The observer of the dance also participates through an identification with the declaration and proclamation of the dancers.

There are many reasons to celebrate God, but in praise dance there does not need to be a reason. The dance is an avenue to celebrate the deep joy of praise. It expresses a joy that wells up for both the dancers and observers. We praise him for who he is, not for his actions on our behalf. In all forms of sacred dance, the declaration of great joy and thanksgiving to God is the statement made by the dancers.

There is a definite style of dance that I call praise dance. The steps in praise dance are lively, with many hops, skips, jumps, and claps. There are many quick Israeli steps like the *mayim, hora* and *tcherkessia*, which lend themselves to fast dances. Arms are often raised in a gesture of thanksgiving to God. The quickness of praise dance lends itself to joy and enthusiasm, which is contagious for both dancers and congregants. The dance is not only our joyous response to the music but also to the words of the songs. When we are comfortable with the dances, we will concentrate on the lyrics of the praise songs. I encourage the dancers to sing the songs as they dance in order to enter completely into the total experience of praise and worship.

Like prayer, our voices and dances communicate to the very throne of God. As we enter into deep worship, our spirits are humbled in submission to God's sovereignty, but there is also a passionate response to his love in our hearts. The act of dancing becomes a true expression of giving our bodies as a living sacrifice unto God (Romans 12:1).

Praise dance brings out an exuberance of celebration that allows us to fully give ourselves to God. Like children, who are able to express their feelings with total abandonment, praise dance gives us an opportunity to exercise our hearts, souls, and might in blessing towards God. Even the church father, Jerome (340–420 c.e.), recognized that prayerful dance was "good and essentially joyful in its expression of praise."[1] Many other famous church fathers also felt that dance would bring one's bodily members into accord with the love of God. The 17th century Hasidic Jewish movement employed dance to elicit joy from people whose life was often desperately poor and difficult. It was their way to let dance create spiritual joy out of human misery.

When our congregation first allowed dance during the

service, I was a little skittish. I feared that with only a small portion of the congregation able to dance, the majority of non-dancers in the congregation would be upset. I assumed they would feel left out or grow tired of watching others have so much fun. My fears were unwarranted. I came to understand the dynamic of congregational dance in a new way.

Just as we love to see people celebrating life, the congregants enjoy watching the dancing people praise with their whole hearts. It is similar to the joy we feel as parents when we watch our children gleefully enjoy something new. This is the experience of those who impressionably watch and joyfully participate in the fullness of praise and joy within the dance.

Those who observe the dance are often as much participants as those who are dancing. Although they are not physically moving, the dance communicates feelings and experiences that make them feel included in the devotional act. Observers discover their worship is heightened to a point where their hearts become softened toward God. I learned that observers enjoy a new sense of openness before the Lord.

Last year I began learning to play the drums. I had always wanted to learn, so I just set my mind to it. The most demanding task was to get to a place where I felt comfortable with my skill level, so that I could really enter into worship without being self-conscious about my playing. If I never got to the point of being able to worship, I would have stopped playing altogether.

One day, while playing with the worship team, things just clicked and I was able to enter into worship while playing the drums. Now I appreciate even more the skill of our regular drummer. This illustration applies equally to dance. Not everyone is secure with their sense of rhythm and physical coordination. Other people find that they are too self-conscious to worship in this fashion. Yet everyone can participate and be blessed through observing others as they dance. We all appreciate skilled performers worshipping God. In fact, our worship experience can be enhanced by watching others.

The dance team leads the congregants into worship, just as the worship team does with their instruments. As each person in the congregation finds the best personal means to participate in the worship, a strong spiritual harmony results, a wonderful sense of God's *Shekhinah* (glory) or presence, and a oneness in the Spirit. The rest of the congregation are not just observing, but joining in with raised voices. While the dancers dance, the congregation claps and sings along. There is a dance in every pair of feet as there is a song in every heart, even for the person who does not know the words or the steps.

I will never forget how dance began in our first congregation back in 1987. I had just returned from my first trip to a Messianic Rabbis' conference in Philadelphia. While there, I saw first-hand how Messianic dance could be a blessing. Although I had experienced every style of praise and worship I could imagine, I had never experienced anything like this! That weekend at Beth Yeshua Messianic Synagogue changed my spiritual life. I did not know how to incorporate what I saw there in my congregation, but I knew that I had to try. Starting the next week, my wife and I began to teach some dances after the service in the fellowship hall. I was not too surprised to see the people's enthusiasm. After six or seven weeks, we all became better dancers, learning the basic steps.

One week, while I was looking at the songs that we would do that Shabbat in the service, I realized that we had learned one of the dances for one of them. A prompting from the Lord came to me that we should dance in the service. This would be a radical step. With fear and trepidation I said "Yes" to the Lord.

I was concerned that people would think it sacrilegious to dance during the service. It was one thing to dance after services during fellowship time, but to dance during the actual praise and worship could upset many people. I also knew that Jewish people were not used to dancing in traditional synagogues.

As you can imagine, there was a whole new anointing of praise poured out that Shabbat that has continued and spread for eight years. Every time a Jewish person visits our congregation, they are impressed with the lively, spirited, enthusiastic dancing. This is the true proclamation of praise dance. Jewish visitors tell us that they wish their synagogue would dance during the service too, then they might go more than twice a year.

Visitors to our congregation are usually amazed when the music begins. Thirty or forty people, men and women, boys and girls of all ages rise from their seats and begin to dance with such exhilaration that you would think you were in the middle of a wedding celebration. I am told that the first question that usually comes to mind is, "Why are these people so excited?" But the answer is soon apparent. Our people know their God and want to give him praise and thanksgiving. It is difficult to come to the congregation with the weight of the world on your shoulders and make it through the praise time without releasing that weight. This is why we look forward so enthusiastically to each Shabbat, knowing the power of praise to lift our burdens and fill us with the joy of the Lord.

One of the joys of having a well-developed dance ministry is the opportunity to do outreach ministry using dance. We go to malls, parks, beaches, anywhere that people gather. We also look for

Dance outrteach in Tel Aviv, Israel

areas in which to meet Jewish people and Israelis. I have noticed that praise dances, whether Messianic or Israeli, cause people to stop and watch. In a world with so little joy, they receive our ministry whether they understand it or not. Sometimes we can see their faces change as they catch our contagious joy.

While some of us are dancing, many others of our congregation come to share the reason for their joy—Yeshua the Messiah. By the time a person has enjoyed the dance, received information about our congregation and the Lord, or received prayer, their life can be radically changed. Our congregants will walk through an area sharing who we are and often have opportunities to pray with people. Usually one or two people receive Yeshua as Messiah at these outreaches.

Dance Outreach in Kfar Giladi, in the Galilee region of Israel

The Body of Messiah is just beginning to understand the power of praise. Praise through dance not only changes our congregations, but can help us reach a dying world for Yeshua the Messiah.

DANCE AS WORSHIP

Carolyn Deitering, in her book on liturgical dance, explains how the dances of praise lead us into the dances of worship. She says, "The dancer is the dance is the joy. Hence, if a dancer is responding to God, he or she, simply by dancing, enters into a communion with the deity and manifests a worshipful response: the dance is the worship."[2] The glorious joy of praise helps us to release the weight of our personal circumstances in order to come to God with all of our heart, soul, and might so that we are prepared to praise and worship the Lord.

Once established in the ambiance of praise, we are able to break through our personal spiritual barriers and worship God in spirit and in truth. Sacred dance can lead us into the very presence of God, causing us to worship him with more richness and intimacy than ever before.

The Hebrew understanding of the human being does not separate the physical body from the mind or soul. The person can be one choreographed expression of intimacy toward and with God. In Judaism, worship has always been denoted by simple movements such as bending the knee or bowing. The ancient *Aleinu* prayer includes the words, "We bend the knee and bow before the King of Kings." Worship is our submission before an awe-inspiring God. We put our complete trust in him without hypocrisy. We forget our own circumstances and lose ourselves in him.

In worship dance, the steps move very slowly. The arms are lifted up one or two at a time in a reverential manner. There are many worship movements like the coupe, cross-overs, hands lifted in worship, brush steps and bowing that lend themselves to worship. A dance called *Hallelujah* is done holding hands in a circle and includes a cross-over step that enables the dancer to bow as his hands move up and then down. It is a very powerful time of receiving the mercy and lovingkindness of the Lord.

As you grow from the awkward stages of dance novice, past the stage when you feel like a *klutz* (a Yiddish term for an uncoordinated person), to the point of being focused on the Lord without being self-conscious, you will find a whole new avenue of worship opening before you.

When I began to dance, I felt so clumsy that I could not imagine doing it in front of anybody. Once I became more comfortable with the dances, I was able to move into a closer intimacy with God and to express that love through dance. I was no longer concerned with others watching me. People would tell me what a blessing my dancing had been. Many times I have wished that the worship time would never end. The awareness of our majestic, future dancing in heaven before the throne of God has become a very real experience for me.

Praise dances enable us to be filled with an overwhelming joy in the Lord. I have found that worship dances allow me to experience an intimacy with the Lord. As I learn more steps and dances, I continue to find many new ways to express the joy and love of God through dance.

5

FORMS AND STYLES OF
SACRED DANCE

In ancient Israel, King David used dance to unite his community and train his soldiers. We rarely think of worship as building up our community in such practical ways. But our word "liturgy" dates back to a Latin word, *leitourgia*, first used to designate "the public work that a person did in order to help build and repair roads and bridges and to do other public works for the community."[1]

Our service in the liturgy of worship is a visible, practical enterprise except that it builds invisible bonds between the individual worshippers and, more important, between the worshipper and God. Both Peter (1 Peter 2:4, 5) and Paul (Ephesians 2: 21, 22) allude to this picture when they speak of the body of believers being "built up" together as "living stones" with Yeshua as the "chief cornerstone." Whether it is in praise to God, or worship to assist the congregants to experience the presence of God, Messianic dance is a means to build up your worship community.

In every culture, dance is a leading expression of community life. Each culture has historically reinterpreted dance, developing those forms and styles which meet its growing social needs. Doug Adams points out that believers have a communal tradition of sacred dance. He suggests, "surveying the Jewish and Christian records, we can see that communal rather than individual dancing is the norm for worship....there was no individual dance to God in pure Israelite practice."[2] A quick overview of the history of Jewish biblical dance confirms this insight.

In ancient Israel, dance incorporated Middle Eastern nomadic forms into choreographed circle and line dances. Later, during the Second Temple period, around the time of Yeshua, dance was historically used by the Israelites within the Temple precincts for sacred ritual narration. The references concerning dance in the Talmud (the codified body of Jewish tradition and teaching—circa 500 c.e.), indicate that dances were all communal in nature. Sacred dance was viewed as a community statement.

I want to stress that sacred dance as a communal expression does not preclude other forms of dance as valid forms of worship. I am trying to establish a foundation for a particular philosophy centered in the revival of congregational dance that is rooted in the biblical and historical faith of Israel.

Modern Israelis have adapted the popular steps of Israeli folk dance to celebrate traditonal themes. When Israel became a nation in 1948, many of the ancient folk dances became a part of the national, Zionist expression of their community. Today, Israeli dance is a contemporary living expression of religious worship that brings us back to the Judeo-Christian roots of our faith.

The Messianic movement has employed and reinterpreted Israeli folk dance forms as the foundation of its praise and worship. It is a form of community expression, and in worship it is nothing less than a communication with God, like prayer. Sacred dance is prayer in motion. We are using our bodies to accentuate the words of our lips as they ascend to heaven.

Messianic dance is generally done in the form of a circle or line dance, but other forms of dance can be used. There is a popular Israeli dance called *Ki Eshmera* which is a prayer that invokes God to watch over us as we honor his Sabbath. By the time we finish dancing this lovely dance, we actually feel the presence of

God blessing our Sabbath rest.

Dance is also a vehicle for Scripture to be narrated. An example is the Israeli dance, *Lechu N'rananah*. This dance narrates the story of a traditional Israeli family preparing for the *Shabbat*. It is a marvelous dance that encourages us to honor and welcome the Sabbath.

Another form of dance is the proclamation dance. In the proclamation form of dance, narrative Scripture is dramatized allowing the participants to become more integrally involved with the Word of God by physically acting out its truths. Several Israeli and Messianic dances incorporate the *Shema*. Taken from Deuteronomy 6:4–11, the *Shema* is a powerful, traditional prayer that has been central to Jewish worship for thousands of years. It includes this command: "You shall love the Lord your God with all your heart, soul, and might" (Deuteronomy 6:5). Surely, dance is a wonderful expression of that very ordinance.

There is something very practical, as well as theological, in this command to love God with our whole being. Our English versions of the Bible frequently use the word "soul" as a translation of the Hebrew word, *nephesh*, which refers to a "living being." Although modern Hebrew uses the word *guf* to designate the human body in general, in the Bible, the word *guf* refers only to dead bodies. There is actually no biblical Hebrew term for a soul without a body. A person is referred to as a *nephesh*. The ancient Israelites never considered a body as an organism to be alive without a spiritual component. As one commentator put it, "this is because the Old Testament writers did not feel the need to refer to the bodily organism considered by itself. Indeed, they did not regard a person as a sum of parts but as a unitary being."[3] Unlike the Greek concept of a soul trapped within a body, the Hebrew concept is of an animated soul and body in conjunction—heart, soul, might. The act of dancing is a visible presentation of this Scripture, with all the aspects of our physical and spiritual being in unity worshipping the Creator.

The processional dance is one of the most ancient and

popular examples of dance. Dating back to the eleventh century, the church used the *tripudium*, or "threshold" processional dance for congregants to enter and leave the sanctuary. Standing five to ten abreast, the congregants took three steps forward and then one step back, processing through the doors to the front of the sanctuary. This was a means of establishing a sense of oneness as the church came together. A similar recessional took place at the end of the service, with the congregants doing this little dance until they were all outside of the door. The processional gave the people a sense of oneness as they went out into the world. Today, in most liturgical churches, you can see the holdover of the processional as the priest, acolytes, and other leaders process to the altar.

In Jewish synagogues, when the Torah is taken out of the Ark, there is a processional around the sanctuary with the Torah. As the Torah is carried aloft, the congregants show honor for the Word of God by either kissing their fingertips or their Bibles and then touching the Torah with them. Each year at the national conference of the Messianic Jewish Alliance of America, the Friday evening

Torah procession in a Messianic synagogue

service is preceded by a fabulous processional of banners with choreography. Participants of all ages and backgrounds from around the world make a processional around a large hall several times accompanied by singing, the blowing of the *shofar* and special dances.

Meditation dance quiets the soul for a closer communion with God. It is a dance form made up of reasonably simple and repetitive steps that allow the participants to concentrate on the Lord, rather than on their steps. One of these is a Messianic dance called *A Resting Place*, which is simple and sweet. When an integral member of our community passed away a few years ago, we performed this dance at the graveside service. This was the first time I had seen a dance done at a funeral. The audience was asked to meditate upon the deceased and his strong faith in God while we performed this beautiful dance. It was truly one of the most powerful experiences of my life. There was not a dry eye in the group. Everyone testified for weeks afterwards about the powerful presence of God during that dance.

There are dances of repentance, too. These dances help bring us to a place of humility and confession before God. One Messianic dance called *Fall Upon Us Now* incorporates these words

> We and our fathers have sinned against your name,
> forgotten to honor the source of Israel's fame...

While these words are sung, the dancers' repentance is represented with worshipful steps that bring the soul back to a place of brokenness and submission to the Almighty.

Any discussion of dance forms must include celebration dances. The Messiah's reinterpretation of the Passover covenant meal with his disciples was brought into the church as the Eucharist or Communion rite. Dating from the 2nd century, the apocryphal Acts of John represents the followers of Yeshua breaking bread and drinking of wine as celebrated by dancing. In the Middle Ages, the church celebrated the Eucharist with a circular processional around the table of the Lord. Participants would come to the table of the Lord corporately in this choreographed fashion. In our congregation, I find that the processionals to and from the table of the Lord (*Shulkhan Adonai*) become powerful times of meditation, reflection, and prayer.

In Messianic communities we do not speak of our new believers going through baptism, but use the original Jewish term *mikveh* (immersion). The mikveh is a time of purification, proclamation and renewal for the believer. Mikveh services in our congregation are naturally followed by a time of praise and thanksgiving in both song and dance.

The church has a long history of incorporating dance into the sacrament of baptism. Louis Backman states:

> Hippolytus (third century) connected the dancing figures of the Old Testament with the allegorical dances of the Christ...continuing such customs as the dance to the baptismal font.[5]

Ambrose, Bishop of Milan, (340–397 C.E.) tells how baptismal candidates would approach the font with dancing steps. The celebration of new life in Messiah was expressed in dance. Dancing for joy is a perfect response to the "new birth."

Most important among the celebration dances are the various holiday dances. Each holiday incorporates dance into the remembrance and retelling of its origins. For *Simchat Torah*, rejoicing with the Torah includes dances of thanksgiving to God for his *Torah*, or Word. *Sukkot*, the Feast of Tabernacles, includes traditional thanksgiving dances for the harvest. Even during the Second Temple period, the *Mishnah* tells how the most respected men of the community performed the ritual torch dance in the Temple precincts, while the women filled the galleries to watch.

Torches were waved and tossed into the air accompanied by the Levite choir and musical instruments.[6]

At the conclusion of this feast, during the time of Yeshua, the priests led a special rite of water-drawing from the pool of Siloam. This rite was accompanied with joyous dancing which represented the fervent desire of the nation for the coming of Messiah and his kingdom. The Talmud says about this feast, "He who has not seen the rejoicing at the place of the water-drawing has never seen rejoicing in his life."[7] The Gospels record that Yeshua stood up during the celebration to declare, "If any man is thirsty let him come to me and drink" (John 7:37).

In addition to the dances for this holiday, the number of special dances for men, women, and children is extensive and includes ancient *Shavuot* (Pentecost) harvest dances, coronation dances for *Rosh HaShanah* (New Year), and fun, light-hearted dances for *Purim*, the festival of Esther.

Our list of celebration dances is far from exhaustive. The subject is far too broad for us to include all the numerous forms of national Israeli folk dances that tell stories of the *chalutzim*, the pioneers of Israel. Neither do we have space here for all of the rites of the ancient Sephardic Israelis, or the acts of remembrance by Ashkenazi Jews who escaped Hitler's diabolical final solution. Israel's nationalism, patriotism and deliverance by God's hand are proclaimed in every area of her cultural life, including dance.

Every generation reinterprets dance to express its beliefs and values. Sacred dance in Israel has developed, through these various forms, to bring the presence of God into the community of faith. Whether in a Jewish or Christian context, the forms have intermingled with one another throughout history. In our time, the Spirit of God is moving in a very gracious way again to bring renewal to the body of believers, both Jew and non-Jew. Following the leading of the Spirit, the Messianic movement is leading the way in developing the many forms of dance to express praise, worship, and the proclamation of God.

6

UNDERSTANDING MESSIANIC DANCE STYLES

There are several styles of Israeli and Jewish cultural dance that make up the essential forms used in the Messianic movement. The three most popular forms are represented by Israeli folk, Yemenite and Hasidic styles. All three have greatly influenced today's Messianic dance revival and contributed different flavors and cultural nuances.

ISRAELI FOLK DANCE

The first style of Israeli dance is the traditional *Israeli folk* dances that have become the foundation of Messianic circle dances. This style is made up of the basic *yemenite, mayim, hora,* and *tcherkessia* steps. These rudimentary steps make up the basic choreography of Israeli circle dances.

Popular Israeli folk dances have their roots in ancient biblical Israel and were developed by brave pioneers who rebuilt the state of Israel. Long before 1948, when Israel officially became a nation, these early visionaries farmed the desert by day and danced by night. The national spirit—a spirit that called Jewish people from around the globe to give birth to a new nation—is embodied in Israeli folk dance. When Israel became a nation, the whole country celebrated God's deliverance of his people through dance.

Both religious and secular Jews perceive God as the power and will behind the rebirth of the state of Israel. They understand God as the deliverer of his covenant people who have been given stewardship of his land. Israeli folk dances proclaim God's faithfulness to his covenant, his Torah, his land, and his people.

The vibrant spirit of thanksgiving to God and praise for his deliverance is embedded in the character of Israeli folk dance. Folk dances are popular local expressions of a cultural passion and vision. By nature, they will normally be simple, easily learned steps. The simplicity of these folk dance steps makes it possible to quickly learn the vocabulary and acquire a proficiency in Messianic dance.

YEMENITE DANCE

The second form of dance is the Yemenite dance. This form is culturally rooted in the semitic cultures of Arabia and North Africa. This traditional style of bouncy, assertive steps is commanding by nature. Male dancers especially enjoy these dances.

The Yemenite influence is pervasive in all aspects of Israeli culture today. In 1952, *Operation Magic Carpet* repatriated many Yemenite Jews to the land of Israel. They brought with them their vivacious, colorful traditions of music and dance which are related to the Arab culture that is so much a part of Israel and its surroundings. The Sephardic Jews have infused Israel with a cultural vitality that has grown in popularity along with their increase in numbers.

The Yemenite style of dance is currently very popular in Israel and is having a resurgence among Israeli dancers. The Messianic movement is also assimilating Yemenite steps into Messianic choreography. There is a sense of oriental antiquity that is inherent in this form of dance. The bouncy steps are strong and effective in praise and spiritual warfare dances. The vibrant steps and infectious rhythms make it hard to stay in your seat. The

Yeminite dancing is performed in costume Beth Emunah Messianic synagogue.

sounds of *ululation* (the rapid clicking sound of the tongue hitting the roof of the mouth) that accompany these songs lift and strengthen the spirit.

HASIDIC DANCE

The third form of Jewish dance is Hasidic in origin. This cultural style developed over the last few hundred years by Jews living in the cultural greenhouse of the *shtetl*, the small Eastern European Jewish communities. In their resistance to assimilation, these European, or Ashkenazi, Jews developed a style of music and dance that reflects the bittersweet soul of the *diaspora* (exile). At times, the music is filled with the joy of thanksgiving for election and safety as a community. Other times, there is the haunting melodic longing for deliverance and the coming of Messiah.

Restrained, and constraining in movement, the traditional *klezmer* step is very popular in Messianic choreography. The shuffling steps and movements in and out of the circle help define this style of dance. The arms are often hand-in-hand over the shoulder, or hand on each other's shoulders.

For many, these dances traditionally represent Jewish culture—a picture of men with *pe'ot*, or side curls, dancing in lines and circles together to *klezmer* music. A majority of Jewish people relate to this cultural expression both in Israel and elsewhere. Just as this religious culture has shaped perceptions of Judaism at large, so also has this style of music and dance had some of the strongest influence on Jewish and Israeli dance.

Beyond these three main types of cultural dance styles, there will naturally be local diversity among various countries and subcultures within countries. The dances of Israel will continue to be infused with new styles of dance as more Jews return to Israel from other countries. The Scriptures tell us that God will continue to call his people back to Israel from the four corners of the earth. Over the last decade, Russian immigration has vastly increased their numbers and created an influential presence in Israel. Lately, the Ethiopian airlift known as *Operation Moses*, has brought thousands of Jews from that country. We can expect to see more new influences and diverse dance from these cultures.

The Messianic movement also enjoys integrating diverse cultural expressions. For example, during a recent Messianic Jewish Alliance national convention there was a visiting group of Messianic dancers from Monterey, Mexico. While they danced the *hora* and other traditional Jewish dances, they used a unique swinging arm motion over the head in a circle and a distinctive turn with the hand behind the back. Their steps seemed quick and deliberate. This style reflects traditional Mexican and Spanish dances. Small cultural differences like these enable various cultural nuances to continually bring new vitality into Messianic dance.

Although there is room for cultural diversity within the styles and forms of Messianic dance, it is important for Messianic dance to retain the continuity of our Israeli, Jewish cultural and biblical roots. I believe that continuity is important to Messianic dance for three reasons: unity, witness, and heritage.

UNITY

First, I believe that there needs to be a unity in Messianic dance that knits together Messianic congregations throughout the world. Wherever a Messianic believer goes, they should be able to participate in the local dance ministry. Messianic liturgy and music has developed from similar Israeli and Jewish roots and has a familiarity no matter what the surrounding culture. Every region of the country will have some diversity in style. But if the basic steps that are the foundation of Messianic dance are maintained, there will still be general consistency. This is especially important with Messianic dance as it is transferred into local churches. It might be easier for a church to begin with Messianic dance and then to develop its own style. I firmly believe that it is important for the church to be in continuity with the basic styles and philosophy of Messianic dance.

WITNESS

The character of Messianic dance also allows us to have effective outreach. Jews and Israelis identify with our dances whenever we go to a park, shopping mall, or beach for an evangelistic outreach. We usually perform a variety of dances from each of the cultural styles that make up Israeli dance. This strikes a familiar cord with American Jews, whether Ashkenazi or Sephardic, as well as with people from many other cultural backgrounds.

Another aspect of dance outreach is not so much evangelistic but informational. Often, we are asked to educate churches about our ministry and the Jewish roots of their faith. When we go to these churches, we are able to share the heritage we have as Messianic believers. The Jewish, biblical roots of our Messianic faith are at the heart of the rich heritage we share with the churches.

Continuity in dance also gives a strong witness to our local Jewish communities. No matter what style of dance is familiar to our community, we should demonstrate that style. For instance, if we live in Mexico, we should adopt the Messianic dances with more of a Mexican flavor. In doing so, we are better able to speak to our community. Since Messianic dance is such a potent tool for evangelism, we must speak in our cultural context as effectively as possible. That does not mean that if we live in Yemen that we could only dance in a Yemenite style. But we should not seek to invent some style of Messianic interpretive dance that is totally foreign to our community.

Messianic dancing attracts attention in a Venice Beach evangelistic outreach.

I personally enjoy special performances of interpretive Messianic dance. Interpretive dance is also a very popular expression of faith. However, if a Messianic congregation uses interpretive dance as their primary style of congregational dance, that congregation will lose much of its cultural rootedness in and witness to its community. Likewise, any church that becomes involved in Messianic dance should also have a heart to reach the Jewish community and should explore its Jewish heritage.

HERITAGE

The last reason for continuity is our spiritual heritage, which is why we dance. We express through dance the biblical roots of our faith in Messiah. Romans 11 says that the faith of our fathers, and the covenant he made with them, is the root by which the wild olive branches have become attached to something that is ancient and biblical. The Messiah, Yeshua, was born, ministered and gave his life for us in this context. He came to bring salvation to the lost sheep of the house of Israel, first, and then to all the nations. It is important that Jewish and Israeli cultural expressions be a continual part of our praise and worship.

We have seen historically how the church cut itself off from its Jewish roots. In severing its Jewish heritage, much of the spiritual nutrition of the church's faith has been lost over the centuries. Now God is again restoring the entire body of Messiah through these Jewish, biblical roots with a rich culture of tradition and joy. Messianic dance is not just a Jewish phenomenon. It is a picture of the resurrection life of Yeshua expressed today in its biblical and historic context.

7

THE TRANSFORMING POWER OF DANCE

Dance is a life-transforming experience. It is not only an expression of praise and worship, but a means by which the transforming power of the presence of God can be received by the believer. Through dance, God gives us access to his presence in order to transform us. It is part of the maturing process that follows salvation and redemption in Yeshua. As the disciples of Yeshua were described as having been with him, so we also become his witnesses as we are changed by his presence.

When Yeshua died and made atonement for us, we received the promise of full transformation and healing. This change is available to us today in the name of Yeshua. The prophet Isaiah said,

> *But he was wounded for our transgressions, he was bruised for our iniquities; the chastisement of our peace was upon him; and with his stripes we are healed* (Isaiah 53:5).

When we come to Yeshua we receive forgiveness of sin, and we enter into a process of growing in him for the remainder of our lives. The transformation which takes place is the healing reality of the kingdom of God, inherent in our salvation. This healing includes a spiritual return to the Lord, an emotional healing from wounds, and a recovery from physical afflictions.

There are many avenues for healing in our lives. The first is the Word of God. As we read and absorb the Word of God into our lives, we find ourselves receiving greater healing. We become more like him in whom we have put our faith—Yeshua, our healer. King David says, "He sends his word, and heals them, and delivers (them) from their destructions" (Psalm 107:20).

A second important avenue for healing is prayer. In the intimacy of our communication with God, we hear his voice and obey his words. Our lives are then changed in accordance with his will. Day by day, Yeshua is formed within us, making us that promised new creation.

A third avenue for healing and transformation is praise and worship, which releases the transforming power of God in our lives. When we express devotion and trust in God through praise and worship, we experience the change that results from being in the glorious presence of God. The more that we can be clean and open vessels of worship, the more God can manifest his presence in and through our lives. Dance can be an important element of praise and worship that releases healing and transforms us. In the act of dancing, we become channels of adoration to God. As dancers before the Lord, we are called to submit our will to him so that he may more and more fully use us as a royal priesthood in intercession for our congregation.

In the last few years, there has been a new phenomenon of intercessory prayer through dance. A number of believers involved in intercessory prayer have begun to use dance as a medium of intercession. I have not personally experienced this avenue of sacred dance, but I can imagine it as a very powerful vehicle for God's hand to move through and for his people.

A couple of years ago a very close friend and participant in our dance team became ill. While we worshipped with his favorite dance, we all interceded in prayer for him. It was a mighty time of intercession in dance. When we come together in submission to God's will through intercession and worship before his throne, the Spirit of God is forcefully present in the midst of the congregation in praise and worship.

The most important avenue for healing is the total redemption of the individual from the spiritual bondage of this world. As lost sheep, we have strayed far from the creator of our souls. At the moment of salvation, God begins to direct us away from the destructive paths of our lives and sets us free to return to him. This radical work of salvation through repentance is the most important healing in our lives. We are released from the power of sin that has kept us in bondage. This healing is a very broad work of God's grace in which we appropriate the dynamic change that is available through Yeshua's atonement. Here as well, dance can be an important tool to bring about healing and transformation.

The power of God's redemptive healing power through dance is evident whenever we do outreach. In the information age, believers find it more and more difficult to connect on a personal level with people in their communities. A believer standing on a street corner passing out tracts is viewed as an affront by many— perhaps rightly so. They may be seen as someone who does not interact with the needs or concerns of their audience. Dance is a public activity, and invites the onlooker to share—to partake of the joyful celebration. As we lead in dance outreaches in our community, the Spirit of God calls us to minister the healing of his love.

Each summer we have taken our dance outreach team to the worst area of Seattle for outreach. On Saturday night the streets are full of interesting people. The atmosphere of depression, oppression and fear is always thick. We felt that the Lord spoke to us specifically that we were to bring joy into that sad environment. In the midst of that degradation came a refreshing presence that brought and peace. I saw people who were depressed and confused have their lives radically changed by our outreach and the word of redemption.

When unbelieving people come to our congregation for the

first time and see the joyful worship expressed by the dance, they experience the love of God in a new form. They are open to experience God in new ways, to return to him and to be healed in the name of Yeshua. Through Messianic dance, many people are able to hear that call for the first time.

Dance has always been a mighty tool of spiritual power and warfare. In the story of Jehoshaphat's battle against the kings of Ammon, Moab, and Mount Seir, he sent the praising, worshipping and dancing children of Israel out before the soldiers (2 Chronicles 20:20–23). This is one of the clearest examples of how God uses sacred dance as a form of spiritual warfare.

Messianic dance is an arena for spiritual warfare and deliverance. Something happens to us in the spiritual realm when dancers submit to God their body, soul, and might. When we dance as a form of spiritual warfare, we are waging a heavenly battle here on earth. The battle against the power of sin in our lives is usually the first battlefield. I have seen very immediate and convincing deliverance over demonic forces in people's lives through dance.

I remember a young woman who started attending one of our congregations. She was a relatively new believer who often acted erratically. She had problems in the congregation, especially in relationships with other congregants. Many of us began to sense that she needed release from some powerful bondage that she had brought with her into the faith. While we were waiting and praying for an opportune time to approach her, we noticed a change in her demeanor. Clearly, an internal battle was taking place. Some days she would have a supernatural peace; other days her behavior was almost uncontrollable.

I will never forget the day that she learned one particularly powerful spiritual warfare dance. That dance was pivotal in the transformation of her life. The dance is called Joshua, and is a traditional dance about Joshua taking the promised land and having victories over the Kings of Caanan. The dance is very forceful and enables the dancer to have victory over spiritual enemies. As this woman danced that dance, I noticed her entire countenance change dramatically. From that day forward there was a noticeable change in her attitude toward ministry and toward others. She began to reach out to others in compassion and to find new areas of ministry. Today she is a pillar of her congregation, teaching others about the transforming and delivering power of dance. This woman is just one example of how dance can be a dynamic vehicle of God's healing ministry.

Historically, dance has been practiced by the church as a means of deliverance from the bondage of evil and the devil. Gregory of Nazianzus, Bishop of Constantinople, wrote, "May we flee from all the chains of the devil in performing triumphant ring dances."[1] "Early Christian writings and later hymnody evidence the use of dance to shake off bondage to the devil and disease."[2]

New believers came into the faith from pagan backgrounds and brought with them many spiritual problems. They experienced deliverance through sacred dance and began a transformed, new life of freedom in Messiah. I believe that then, as now, the Spirit of God takes over all the areas of our lives that used to be the territory of the enemy.

In addition to spiritual battles of deliverance and healing, there are battles of the flesh that are also healed through the ministry of dance. People who need to submit areas of their lives to the kingship of Messiah are often changed by their involvement in Messianic dance. Pride, selfishness, fear, guilt, and condemnation are examples of the emotional areas that can go through dynamic spiritual change and healing through dance.

Sometimes in Messianic dance the Lord must reshape our will by enveloping us with a mighty sense of his love. This is part of his molding of a "peculiar people." When a long-time believer experiences this reforming process by the Lord, the results may be just as dynamic as the healing they received when they first came to God.

As a congregational leader, I am constantly in prayer for the metamorphosis of peoples' lives. After more than twenty years of ministry, I can attest to the fact that Messianic dance is a very effective tool to bring about change in people's lives. As individuals in your congregation continue to learn and grow in the Lord, you will also witness mighty healings.

Less visible, but just as important, are healings in the deep places of the heart which may have caused a believer to struggle for many years. These areas may be the most difficult to be healed, and the fiercest battles for the spiritual life of the believer may be taking place here. A healing in this area may be a tremendous victory of God. With fresh healings in these areas, believers become more effective in using their spiritual gifts. Those who walk close to the Lord with the confidence of being fully redeemed are the most com-petent ambassadors in ministries of redemption and reconciliation.

There are also emotional healings that take place in the lives of people who enjoy Messianic dance. I have seen change in many believers who struggled with traumatic relationships with family or friends. Through Messianic dance, they found an ability to release themselves in praise and worship which brought them wonderful healing. I do not recommend dance in place of counseling or therapy, but I have found that dance is a very powerful avenue of release and healing that enhances other mechanisms of emotional healing. Dance allows us to physically express our experience of spiritual battles, victories, joys, and sorrows. As a result, we become better servants and witnesses for him.

A very real and debilitating type of disorder is depression. I have seen many believers "put on the shelf" spiritually for extended periods of time due to acute depression in their lives. Messianic dance is very potent in healing us from depression. I have experienced this healing personally.

There was a two month period in my life when I went through a deep depression. I am sure that many have had a similar occasion in their lives, too. During that time I read the words of King David with much empathy, "Why art thou cast down oh my soul, and why art thou disquieted in me?" (Psalm 42:5) A sense of helplessness overwhelmed me and I seemed to lose all hope. I felt that I might never know God's presence and lovingkindness again. Guilt, pain, and fear were my only reality.

During that dark time of depression I often danced before the Lord with my whole heart crying out in anguish. Every time I danced I found God reaching down to me with his love. My dances were very much like King David's prayers of agony that connected him to his heavenly father beyond the normal exchange of words, songs, or liturgy. As I began to dance with deep suffering and torment in my heart, I began weeping with a powerful sense of joy and trust in the unconditional love of God. By the time I finished dancing I had a tremendous release of the Spirit—this is the transforming power of Messianic dance.

People with little confidence in their personal ministry can find within dance a source of healing that helps them to develop spiritually. In the fellowship and camaraderie of dance, they find a non-threatening environment of acceptance where they can develop at their own pace and feel released in their ministry gifts. As opportunities arise to minister in congregational dances and outreach, many people find themselves being stretched and used by God far beyond their boundaries of faith. Their self-esteem grows. Enhanced by the intimacy of praise and worship, they find God healing childhood wounds and hurts.

Those who previously could not even express themselves in worship can find confidence to move into new areas of ministry. They might become capable evangelists, teachers, or leaders within the body of Messiah. This less dramatic, but no less significant aspect of healing takes place through the transforming power of Messianic dance, as God heals, molds, and empowers his people.

The final area of healing through Messianic dance is in the physical realm. Obviously in a ministry where the body is intricately involved, there is a need for physical fitness. We need to be thankful and practice proper health care, yet not be drawn into an attitude that glorifies the body or emphasizes physical ability alone.

I think that most of us have had battles with our weight. Eating disorders and weight problems are the sins of the twentieth century believer. With so many people overweight, dance not only brings a healthy discipline into our lives, but it demands more of the fruit of the Spirit to be manifested. We must give this area of food, weight control, and general health over to the Lord for his scrutiny and healing. I know of several people with weight problems who have found in dance both intimacy with God and a discipline to lose weight. This is obviously not the reason that one gets involved in dance, but it is definitely a benefit.

Beside the natural healing capacity of dance ministry, there are instances of supernatural physical healing through dance. One early Jewish sect called the *Therapeutae* did a dance that was thought to have had the effect of curing diseases. Eusebius (260–340 C.E.), Bishop of Caesarea, testifies to the dance practices of the *Therapeutae* as continuing down to his day.[3] In the Middle Ages healing dances were very popular. A 15th century Catholic hymn that accompanied a dance of healing is as follows:

> Radiating health's
> Wondrous strength,
> He restores to the feeble
> The strength of their limbs!
> He gives to the confused mind
> The gift of reason! (An. Hymn 37:327:9)

As we see in this old hymn, dance was a vehicle for the physical, emotional and spiritual healing of the believer. Dance is a powerful tool with which you can battle the enemy, transform behavior and surrender your whole being into submission to Yeshua, the Messiah.

In the years that I have been involved in Messianic dance, I have seen the transforming power of this effective medium of healing and warfare in action—through restoring and delivering believers, young and old. Growing intimacy with God will create a seed-bed for the growth of the fruit of the Spirit. The capacity to concentrate and focus upon God in worship will cause fears to diminish and a new-found trust to be established. In the dance, burdens may disappear and the weight of problems vanish.

8

HOW TO START A DANCE MINISTRY

I have worked as a rabbi/pastor in full-time ministry for over twenty years. In that time I have become well aware of the common fears that leaders have with a dance ministry. Sometimes a leader is apprehensive that his congregation will be unduly influenced by those who are emotional, experiential, and unsubmitted. This anxiety makes it seem risky for a leader to allow dance in the congregation. Therefore, when believers attempt to start a dance ministry in their congregation they may find that their leaders are unwilling to support the endeavor.

The most important elements of a successful congregational dance ministry are good leadership, organization, and discipline. Although many excellent dance instructors are men, I usually find that the leadership of the dance ministry in a congregation has been filled by a woman. Therefore, I will often refer to "she" in matters concerning the dance leader.

LEADERSHIP

First, I want to discuss the importance of good leadership. Every program needs a champion. Someone who has a vision for the ministry and is willing to work hard to make it succeed. By vision, I mean that the dance leader must have a strong philosophical desire to enable easy entrance to dance by any and all congregants. Her desire must be to make the dance experience an integral part of congregational worship and praise for as many people as possible.

Obviously, the leader must be submitted to the authority of the congregation. She must function effectively both with people above and beneath her in the congregational authority structure.

There must be an urgency within the heart of this champion to teach others how to enter into the joy of dance. The goal of dance leadership is to motivate people within the congregation to become worshippers of the living God, not only dancers. There is a spiritual electricity, a spark present, when an enthusiastic dance leader inspires her dancers. She will encourage them to reach out to people to present a fresh new encounter with the living God and draw people to the Lord.

The dance leader cannot be myopic, having a vision for only the local congregation. She must have a larger perspective for reaching out to the body of Messiah in her entire region and beyond. For this reason, she will always be developing new material, motivated to continue her education in the Messianic movement and Israeli dance.

We are all students in the arena of Messianic dance. The dance leader will benefit from studying with someone who is adept at teaching dance who can show her new dances. Therefore, the dance teacher needs to have a humble and teachable spirit. It is also helpful if she finds a spiritual mentor, someone to act as a prayer partner and sounding board for difficult decisions. Spiritual sensitivity for the direction of the ministry and the people involved is a must. The teachers need to be Spirit-led and Spirit-anointed when communicating vision, curriculum, and devotion.

I want to emphasize that dance is not a performance or exercise, but a powerful form of worship. When two or more are gathered in Messiah's name, there can be fellowship and dance. With inspired leadership, your congregation will find that whenever they get together, the spark of dance will flame up—before and after services, at parties, men's and women's meetings, every time there is opportunity for fellowship. In this manner, dance ministry will heighten the sense of community and fellowship within the congregation. Then, with supportive direction from your congregational leader, the dance ministry will release the power of the Spirit of God and bear good fruit. The dance leader will set the pace for the others. She will communicate the vision, philosophy, and spark that will bring revival to your congregation.

STRUCTURE

Each time I have seen a congregational dance ministry begun, it has been by one person catching the vision. But dance ministry is a team effort. There is too much work for only one person to administer a congregational dance ministry. It often seems that just about the time the leader realizes that she cannot get the dance ministry going alone, God brings alongside just the right person. God will speak to someone who also has a vision for dance ministry and a servant's heart.

It may seem to take forever to train a team sufficiently, but I have found that motivated and enthusiastic people learn quickly. It usually takes six months to a year of intense prayer and training for a basic, good sized team to develop. During this six months or so, a sufficient number of teachers, at least four to six others, can be developed properly to take much of the load off the dance leader.

In order to get a strong dance team to develop to maturity, I have found that it takes about one to one-and-a-half years. The time to develop a dance ministry team varies due to the personalities involved, congregational support, and leadership involvement. God is truly in charge of the dance ministry, and he will bring together the appropriate people to help at just the right time. During this time there will be many opportunities for your faith to be stretched.

The job description of the dance ministry leader may vary, but I would like provide a suggested outline for the position.

Remember, this is the work load of a well-established dance ministry that has a lot of people assisting the leader. She will
- oversee the recruitment and training of teachers
- review dances
- order materials
- duplicate and distribute curriculum for teachers and students
- schedule classes and teachers
- discipline and correct the ministry team when needed.

She will work with the congregational worship leader and worship team to
- develop dance for the services
- choreograph new dances
- develop special holiday performances
- acquire dates and places for outreach.

A team of Messianic dancers minister God's love at the Galleria Mall, in Sherman Oaks, California.

In addition, development of the ministry will require net-working with other dance instructors from both Messianic and non-Messianic groups. This is not an exhaustive list of duties, but it does point out why this needs to be a *team ministry*.

In all the effective dance ministries that I have seen, the leader has delegated most of these jobs to other people who have also caught the vision. Division of labor will make this a very dynamic ministry where many of the congregants can be involved on various levels. Some dance teams have a person who is directly in charge of materials and curriculum, teaching, administering the books, choreography, outreaches, etc. A good organization will enable the ministry to be effective and to grow with the congregation. Overwhelming as this task may seem at first, as with any ministry, you must begin with small steps and allow the Lord to give his direction and anointing as you grow.

The dance leader must maintain a good rapport with the rabbi or pastor of the congregation. She must not only be submitted to his authority, but sensitive to his concerns. A high degree of trust must be established between them. All along the way, there needs to be a willingness to make adjustments and even major changes when necessary.

This is not a static program that can be set in motion by the leadership and then forgotten. It will require time and care from the rabbi or pastor to steer this ministry in tandem with the direction that he senses the Lord moving his particular congregation. No two dance ministries are alike! Each congregation is unique, and its dance ministry will also be unique.

GETTING STARTED

The method that I have found to be the most effective is to start with a weekly beginner's class. Each class follows the same pattern. We always have a time of teaching, sharing, and prayer in every class. The teacher uses this time to share the Messianic vision and lead the people into worship. There is a ten-minute time of teaching and prayer for each dance that is taught. The substance of the teaching can involve the words and meaning of the dance, related Scripture, the Messianic movement, the land or history of Israel, prophecy, or the Jewish roots of their faith. The leader must communicate the sense of worship and prayer that is inherent in the dance. After the teaching, there can be a short time of sharing, followed by a time of prayer.

Every few weeks, the dance leader should teach new, exciting and challenging dances. There is nothing worse than a stagnant worship ministry that performs the same old songs and dances every week. This will motivate the teachers to learn new dances and investigate many other sources. Before they know it, the students will know enough dances and wish to teach others.

After six months or so, you will find several from this first class to be potential teachers. Plan to set up a special time to work with these people at another time during the week, as well as in the beginning classes. It is important to share the vision with them over and over again. If the leader keeps the dance ministry fresh and vital, the new dance teachers will continue to grow rapidly with tremendous enthusiasm. Some of them will catch the vision and want to serve in the dance ministry, too. Before long, they will be able to assist in teaching the beginners' class with the dance leader. In about a year the leader will be able to assign some of them to teach the class.

There are great benefits from sending all potential dance teachers to a regional or national Messianic conference. They will get excited as they experience the dynamic of hundreds of people from all over the world worshipping in dance. I suggest that the congregation pay for the dance leader to go to a yearly conference. She will return with a new sense of excitement and vision that will be translated to the congregation.

In most congregations it is difficult for some people to come out to dance class during the week. Our lives are busy and burdened with many time commitments. One way to solve this problem is to teach a dance class after your main service. If your main service is Saturday morning, teach a beginners' dance afterwards. If you have supplementary meetings on Friday night or Sunday morning, offer classes after those services as well. This enables many more of your congregants to participate and find entry into dance ministry.

After the beginners' class has been going for about a year, you can start an intermediate class for those who have advanced in their skill level. Eventually you will have beginning, intermediate, and advanced classes each week. These classes can be taught by various teachers, while the dance leader spends time working with other teachers and managing the ministry. The possibilities involved through dance ministry might be intimidating, but be assured that it is easier than you think. If you have a vision for dance, just believe that soon other teachers and opportunities will come your way. Since the dance ministry is called of God, it will be carried forward by the Spirit of God.

DISCIPLINE

An important key to the success of any program, especially dance ministry, is good discipline. I know that discipline is difficult for some people, but there can be a lot of abuse and misuse of dance without strong discipline. Some people so enjoy the freedom that dance ministry permits that they do not feel that dance should have restrictions of any kind.

Congregants and dancers need to be taught that dance is choreography, which is by definition a discipline. In the oversight of an effective congregational dance ministry, the dance leader must be willing to confront all types of people. She must not only have an ability to motivate and get along well with others, but have a competence in correcting people. She must be able to render discipline with a tender yet firm hand.

An effective strategy for maintaining discipline should include a monthly meeting with all of the team to discuss programs, policy, and problems. If the vision of the ministry is constantly being placed before the leaders, they will be able to keep perspective when problems arise. They too must learn how to handle awkward situations and problem people.

When I speak to most pastors about dance in the congregation, they have a picture of one or two women in their congregation doing interpretive dance up and down the aisles. In our congregation, we do not allow individual dancing within the congregation.

The basic form of congregational dance is the circle dance. Philosophically, corporate dance is corporate worship, in harmonious celebration under the direction of the music and dance leaders. With the exception of a special performance, the music or dance leaders have the authority to tell a person either playing the tambourine or dancing individually to stop. The dance leader can then encourage them in more appropriate ways to join in. An arm around the shoulder and a few gentle words can correct these problems quickly. After the service the dance leader can take a few more minutes to explain the philosophy of what Messianic dance is all about. I have found that most people want to know how to fit in with the congregational mission.

An appropriate concern that many have regarding dance is the problem of sensuality and temptation. There are many susceptible young people in our congregations who struggle with problems of lust. Dance must not be a stumbling block to those weaker vessels. Temptation is with us always, yet we cannot allow fear to keep us from the blessings of Messianic dance. Therefore, a dance policy concerning dress codes must be adhered to by the dancers and, when necessary, scrutinized by the leaders.

There are social codes that are part of every congregation's style of ministry. If the people see that no one is wearing a miniskirt, tight clothing, halter top, or are dancing without modest dress, they will intuitively get the message. When people get up to dance they are participating in a ministry of the congregation under the proper authority and parameters of that ministry. If they are not appropriately dressed for that ministry they must be corrected.

You will not have any problems with the regulars within the

congregation, because modesty is contagious. Problems will arise with visitors, believers or unbelievers, who are inappropriately dressed and get up to dance. It is best for the leader, after the dance, to casually approach them and again, perhaps with an arm around the shoulder and a gentle word, let them know that their attire is not appropriate for this ministry. Encourage them and say that with the correct attire they would be more than welcome to join the dance. Visitors are usually receptive and do not have hurt feelings. They actually feel more secure when they can trust someone to lovingly correct them.

Another situation that needs immediate correction is the person who either does not know the dance well enough or has a personal style of dancing that is dangerous to other dancers. That person should be exhorted to wait until they learn the dance better or tone down their style so as not to harm anyone.

The key to proper discipline is that no one is stopped from participating, but all are learning how to be more effective in the dance ministry. The Spirit of God is not being stifled, because he desires that everyone participate in harmony. As more and more of your dance leaders learn how to handle situations like these, you will find a strong sense of confidence among the whole congregation. As the dance ministry develops in your congregation, there will be fewer instances of correction, more joy and greater freedom within the bounds of proper discipline.

9

RESOURCES AND NETWORKING

Soon after we developed a commitment to get a large number of congregants to experience worship in dance, we realized the need to develop a new kind of curriculum. If you have ever gone to a Messianic dance class, you may have learned two to four dances that first evening. The next day you tried to remember the dances, but you could not even remember the music. We all know the frustration involved in learning new dances. Since I am a relatively slow learner, I found that each week I had to relearn the dances.

I knew that we had to take another approach in order to accomplish the vision. Since my vision was to make dance as accessible as possible to the greatest number of congregants, some method had to be developed to attain that goal.

First, I put a volunteer in charge of getting copyrights for all the songs and dances that we used in our congregation. Then the dance steps were simply and clearly transcribed on paper so that after each class the students could take home a copy of the steps. I had the music duplicated on fifteen minute tapes. If students learned two dances that first night, they went home with tapes and song sheets with the steps to each of the dances they had learned. The next week, the teacher would quickly review the previous week's dances at the beginning of the class. It was amazing how fast the students learned when they were able to practice during the week at home.

As time went on, the *Messianic Dance International*™ program including these tapes and song sheets was developed. At the beginning of each eight-week dance session the student pays for the class, which includes a tape and a dance booklet with the twelve songs for that session. The booklet includes the dance steps, translation of Hebrew songs, meditations that bring out the Messianic and Israeli contexts and a word study on each song.

The availability of these resources enables new people to quickly learn enough dances to participate in congregational dance worship. With this program, a new participant who attends the classes and is committed to study at home can advance to the level of a skilled intermediate dancer within only six months.

Messianic Dance International™ soon became a resource for many congregations and churches in the Northwest. People involved in dance or wanting dance in their congregations were able to come, learn and take the resource materials back to their own congregations to teach. Congregational dance ministries sprang up in many local churches. Messianic fellowships began their own dance ministries. As committed dance leaders from other congregations began to learn and plant the vision, dance ministries started to blossom all over the area.

We began to receive requests for materials from all over the United States and Canada, and as far away as Israel, Europe, and South America. Everyone wanted videos to go along with the audio tapes, since they were too far away to attend our classes. After a couple of failed attempts, *Messianic Dance International*™ finally made a video to go along with the beginning curriculum. This enabled dance ministries to begin in congregations in Hawaii, Atlanta, Oklahoma, and Los Angeles. As congregations developed their dance ministries, they also began choreographing their own favorite songs as well. Choreography from dance leaders all over the county has been added to our curriculum.

Because there are so many traditional Israeli dances as a part of the *Messianic Dance International*™ curriculum, we also encouraged others to attend local Israeli dance classes or Jewish community centers to dance. *Messianic Dance International*™ is only one source for Messianic and Israeli dance. Your local Israeli dance classes or Jewish community center will not only teach you new dances, but open the opportunity to become more involved in the Jewish community.

In some cities, synagogues and Jewish community centers have asked Messianic dancers to participate with them at holiday events. They sense the excitement and joy of our praise and worship. Paul writes that one of the purposes of our salvation is to make the Jewish people jealous of the spiritual benefits we enjoy (Romans 11: 14). What a great way to reach Jewish people with the good news of Yeshua the Messiah!

NETWORKING

Teachers throughout the United States are able to use the resources of *Messianic Dance International*™ by buying a teacher's kit of master tapes used for classes. This kit goes beyond the initial beginning, intermediate and advanced tape and video series. In the vision that the Lord originally gave to me, I saw a network of dance instructors throughout the country growing and sharing together in the fellowship of dance ministry.

Many dance leaders fly in to see classes and experience dance in our congregation. They get a first-hand look at how a highly developed dance ministry can function. Quarterly dance symposiums are held in the Northwest sponsored by *Messianic Dance International*™. Teachers from all over the region get together to share and pray for dance ministry in their congregations. I would like to see the day when each region has its own networking group of dance teachers. Perhaps a national dance network can be developed.

Messianic Dance International™ resources are a good first step in getting dance established in your community. Involvement in your local Jewish Community Center dance program is another. I think that it is very important for dance leaders to stay in communication and prayer with one another in order to sense what the Spirit of God is doing in your region. In Los Angeles, where there is a very large Israeli population, we have found ourselves much more involved with traditional Israeli dances. Our involvement in the Israeli community is also bearing good fruit for the kingdom.

The demographics and mission may be different in your region, or congregation. You may sense that the mission of your congregational dance ministry is teaching local churches about the Jewish roots of their faith. There are many opportunities to teach and also combat some of the anti-Semitic teachings that have developed in some Christian traditions. As you see, the great thing about a vision borne by God is that it has no end. My vision for Messianic dance ministry goes beyond the dance itself. It is also a tool for outreach to the larger Jewish world and teaching within the whole body of Messiah.

I cannot stress enough the importance of the Father's plan for all his people to get back to the Jewish roots of the faith. But whether your goal is spiritual revival within a congregation, outreach to the Jewish community, or teaching the Jewishness of faith in Yeshua, Messianic dance is a powerful instrument to build up the kingdom of God where he has planted you. After centuries, the spiritual ministry of dance is being restored to the whole body of believers by the Spirit of God.

May your Messianic dance ministry be blessed.

APPENDICES

APPENDIX A
DANCE VOCABULARY

HH	Holding hands
NHH	Not holding hands
CW	Clockwise
CCW	Counter-clockwise
R	Right foot
L	Left foot
Step	Full weight on foot
Step-Hop	Full weight on foot plus a hop on same foot
Mayim	A Hebrew word meaning "water," *Mayim* is a 4-count step, described below.
Mayim to the Right	Moving to the right (CCW), L crosses in front of R. R steps to the right side. L steps behind R. R steps to the right side.

Mayim to the Left	Reverse of above. Moving to the left (CW), R crosses in front of L. L steps to the left side. R steps behind L. L steps to the left side.
Mayim Lift to the Right	L crosses in front of R. R steps to the right side. L steps behind R. Lift R. In fast dances when R is lifted, you hop on L at the same time.
Mayim Lift to the Left	Reverse of above. R crosses in front of L. L steps to the left side. R steps behind L. Lift L. In fast dances when L is lifted, you hop on R at the same time.
Open Mayim to the Right	R steps to the right side (open). L crosses in front of R. R steps to the right side. L steps behind R.
Open Mayim to the Left	Reverse of above. L steps to the left side (open). R crosses in front of L. L steps to the left side. R steps behind L.
Grapevine	Term used in international folk-dancing. Basically like a *Mayim* only without a specific number of counts or steps.
Balance Step(s)	A shift of weight from one foot to another—usually R-L-R-L. Can also be referred to as *Sways*.
Right Yemenite	R steps to the right side. L steps slightly behind R. R steps forward slightly, crossing in front of L. Pause on the fourth count.

Left Yemenite	Reverse of above. L steps to the left side. R steps slightly behind L. L steps forward slightly, crossing in front of R. Pause on the fourth count.
Yemenite Hop	Same as *Yemenite,* but on the fourth count hop instead of pause.
Right Yemenite Hop	R steps to right side. L steps slightly behind R. R steps forward slightly, crossing in front of L. Hop on R.
Left Yemenite Hop	Reverse of above. L steps to left side. R steps slightly behind L. L steps forward slightly, crossing in front of R. Hop on L.
Back Yemenite	Same as *Yemenite Hop,* stepping backwards (either with R or L) instead of to the side.
Right Tcherkessia	Step R forward while lifting L (1st count). Step L back in place (2nd count). Step R backward, while lifting L (3rd count) Step L back in place (4th count). ARM MOVEMENTS: Lift arms above the head on first count, then lower arms for the other three counts, ending with arms hanging down at the sides on the fourth count. When a dance calls for a *Tcherkessia,* it's usually a *Right Tcherkessia.*
Left Tcherkessia	Step L forward, while lifting R (1st count). Step R back in place (2nd count). Step L backward, while lifting R (3rd count). Step R back in place (4th count).

ARM MOVEMENTS: Lift arms above the head on first count, then lower arms for the other three counts, ending with arms hanging down at the sides on the fourth count.

Coupé to the Right

L crosses in front of R, placing weight on L. R steps in place. L steps to the left side, joining R.
ARM MOVEMENTS: With right hand behind the back, left arm follows L as it crosses in front of R. As you step back on R, left arm follows L back to original position at the side.

Coupé to the Left

Reverse of above. R crosses in front of L, placing weight on R. L steps in place. R steps to the right side, joining L.
ARM MOVEMENTS: With left hand behind the back, right arm follows R as it crosses in front of L. As you step back on L, right arm follows R back to original position at the side.

Harmonika

These are *Coupés* with hops added. Each *Harmonika* gets 4 counts.
ARM MOVEMENTS: Hands are usually held.

Harmonika to the Right

L crosses in front of R, placing weight on L. R steps in place. L steps to left side, joining R. Hop on L, raising R slightly off the ground.

Harmonika to the Left

Reverse of above. R crosses in front of L, placing weight on R. L steps in place. R steps to right side. Hop on R, raising L slightly off the ground.

Hora Step Right	R steps to the right. Left toe steps next to R with weight on the left toe. R steps in place (R-L-R, three counts, quick steps).
Hora Step Left	Reverse of above. L steps to the left. Right toe steps next to L with weight on the right toe. L steps in place (L-R-L, three counts, quick steps).
Cross-over to the Right	R steps to the right. L crosses in front of R. Can be followed with R stepping to the right. ARM MOVEMENTS: As you step to the right, raise arms out to side. As L crosses in front of R, bring arms together, cross wrists, and snap fingers.
Cross-over to the Left	Reverse of above. L steps to the left. R crosses in front of L. Can be followed with L stepping to the left. ARM MOVEMENTS: As you step to the left, raise arms out to side. As R crosses in front of L, bring arms together, cross wrists, and snap fingers.
Debka Step	Put right heel forward. Bring R back to join L while lifting L. Put L heel forward. Bring L back to join R while lifting R (heel-step on R; heel-step on L). These are bouncy steps and in some dancing they are done quickly.
Debka Jump	Jump onto both feet, landing with feet slightly apart, while simultaneously turning to the right or left 90 degrees.

APPENDIX B
SAMPLE DANCES

KLEZMER
Traditional Folk Song, Author Unknown
Choreography by Yoav Ashriel
Meditation 1 by Rick Hebron
Meditation 2 by Beverly King
Quotations compiled by Kathy Rosebrook

INSTRUMENTAL
The soul is filled with God as his instruments are skillfully played with hearts of devotion to him

Kathy Rosebrook, 1992

SCRIPTURE SELECTION 1: JEREMIAH 31:33 & HEBREWS 8:10
"But this is the covenant that I will make with the house of Israel after those days," says the Lord: "I will put my law within them, and on their heart I will write it; and I will be their God, and they shall be my people."

MEDITATION 1:
In the 16th century, itinerant Jewish musicians called *klezmers* wandered Europe, blending their musical styles with those of other minstrels of varied backgrounds. The word *klezmer* comes from two Hebrew words: *kle*—a tool—and *zemer*—song or harmony. The idea was that the musician was just a tool used by the music to make itself heard.

About 100 years ago the word came across to America with Jewish immigrants. By this time *klezmer* meant the music or the band that would be present at any gala Jewish event, like a wedding or Bar mitzvah, so the people could dance. We, too, like to dance and, like a wedding, we have chosen a covenant that is worth celebrating. We sing and dance because God has redeemed us and chosen us to be his children. As he promised, he has come to live in our hearts and give us victory over the enemy. We rejoice that *he* has taken away our judgment and cleansed us whiter than snow!

SCRIPTURE SELECTION 2: EPHESIANS 2:10
(ALSO READ EPHESIANS 1:4–10)

For we are of God's making, created in union with the Messiah Yeshua for a life of good actions already prepared by God for us to do.

MEDITATION 2

Jewish worship, education, family life, orchestra, drama, and the joyous, humorous sounds of the itinerant *klezmer* musicians flourished in Eastern Europe despite pogroms, ghettos, and persecutions of all sorts. The themes of the songs which we dance with *klezmer* speak of God's provision, protection, deliverance, and salvation. *Klezmer* takes our thoughts from temporal circumstances and reminds us that God has triumphed.

Before salvation, our lives had no rhyme or reason. Yeshua brought us balance and order. We are God's workmanship, a *poiema* of the Master Designer. God has chosen us to be instrumental in redeeming his creation back to himself and establishing his kingdom.

Each time musicians, dancers, singers, prayers, worshippers, and hearers and doers of the Word "to the praise of his glory" choose to submit to the Lord and to one another, we *proclaim* with our voices, bodies, and lives: Yeshua the Messiah, salvation, is come. It is our privilege as the body of Messiah, the temple of his *Ruakh HaKodesh*, the Spirit of God, to stand in the gap, ministering to God and to each other, and to the world, remembering that in warfare it is God who delivers the wrath, and in blessing it is God who gives the increase. Sing and dance at the triumph of our king!

QUOTATIONS

Music is a universal language, and needs not be translated. With it soul speaks to soul.

B. Auerbach, *Auf der Hohe*, 1865

Music washes away from the soul the dust of everyday life.

B. Auerbach

O Music! miraculous art!... A blast of thy trumpet, and millions rush forward to die; a peal of thy organ, and uncounted nations sink down to pray.

Disraeli, *Contarini Fleming*, 1832

Hidden in a brief adagio there is a sermon on the transient hour;
And lured from inner depths by sweep of bow
May be a vision of the perfect flower,
Immortal blossom of divine intent.
Whose humblest seed explains the firmament.

Lieberman, "Violin Concerto." *NY Times*, Oct. 4, 1953

This song shall testify before them as a witness.

Deuteronomy 31:21

Song is a faithful messenger.

M. Ibn Ezra, *Selected Poems*

The inner history of a people is contained in its songs.

Jellinek. *Der Orient*, 1844

There are melodies that must have words...and melodies that sing themselves without words. The latter are of a higher grade. But these, too, depend on a voice and lips,...hence are not yet altogether pure, not yet genuine spirit. Genuine melody sings itself without a voice. It sings inside, within the heart, in man's very entrails!

Peretz, *Mekubolim*, 1906

> *The individual may pray in prose or even in wordless silence;*
> *a congregation must sing or disband.*
> Abrahams, *Poetry and Religion*, 1920

> *Fear and faith and song go together.*
> Zeitlin, Orot, *HaTekufa*, 1919

> *Every people has its own melody...But Israel sings all of*
> *them, in order to bring them all to God.*
> Abraham Yaakov

DANCE NOTATION
Formation: Circle dance, HH
Level: Beginner

PART 1
1. Four heel-steps to the right (CCW). Put the right heel to the side and put L behind R, bending knees slightly. Palms face out and touch the palms of the people on either side of you.
2. Starting with R go into center of circle, R-L-R-hop, then go backwards L-R-L-hop
3. Two mayims to the left (CW)
4. Coupé to the left (R-L-R) and coupé to the right (L-R-L), then stomp with R next to L.
Repeat #1–4

PART 2
1. Facing the line of direction to the right (CCW), walk forward four steps R-L-R-L. Drop hands and cross them behind you.
2. Touch right heel forward and raise hands to shoulder level. Then touch right toe behind and put hands on hips.
3. Going away from the center of circle (hands still on hips), do a side step (R to side, L behind R and then R to side and

touch withleft heel and snap fingers at waist level)
4. Going back toward center of circle (hands on hips again), do the same step but start with L (L to side, R behind L, L to side and touch with right heel and snap fingers at waist level)

Repeat #1–4

DANCE TEACHING TIPS

Klezmer can be done to many dances. It can also be done in different sequences. In one version of *Klezmer* we do both parts twice and in another one we do Part 1 three times and Part 2 twice. It is fun to shout when you go into the middle of the circle.

CLAP YOUR HANDS

Song by Joel Chernoff
Choreography by Terry Korotkin
Meditation 1 by Kathy Rosebrook
Meditation 2 by Mike and Linda Foster

CHORUS

Clap your hands, all ye people
Clap your hands to the Lord.
Shout unto God with your voice,
A voice of triumph.

VERSE 1

For the Lord Most High is terrible,
He's the great King over all the earth.
He shall subdue the peoples under us,
The nations under our feet.

VERSE 2

Sing praise to our God and King,
For He is King over all the earth.
God reigneth over the heathen,
From His throne in Zion.

VERSE 3

The princes of the people are gathered,
Even God's people of Abraham,
For the shields of earth belong to God,
He is greatly exalted.

CHORUS

Lai, Lai, Lai.........Repeat

SCRIPTURE SELECTION 1: PSALM 66:1–5

Shout joyfully to God, all the earth! Sing the glory of His name; make His praise glorious. Say to God, "How awesome are Thy works! Because of the greatness of Thy power Thine enemies will give feigned obedience to Thee. All the earth will worship Thee, and will sing praises to Thee; They will sing praises to Thy name! Come and see the works of God, who is awesome in His deeds toward the sons of men."

MEDITATION 1

We are a strong and mighty people pursuing our enemies with a shout. We are a peculiar people armed with hands that clap. He has already won the victory! We are triumphant through praising Yeshua the victorious one! God is gone up with a shout (Psalm 47:5), so indeed know he delights in your shouts of triumph unto him.

SCRIPTURE SELECTION 2: PSALM 47
AN ENTHRONEMENT PSALM FOR THE KING OF ETERNITY

Oh clap your hands, all peoples; shout to God with the voice of joy. For the Lord Most High is to be feared, a great and awesome King over all the earth. He subdues peoples under us, and nations under our feet. He chooses our inheritance for us, the glory of Jacob whom he loves. God has ascended with a shout, the Lord with the sound of a trumpet. Sing praises to God, the King of all the earth; sing praises with a skillful psalm. God reigns over the nations; God sits on His holy throne. The prince of the people have assembled themselves as the people of the God of Abraham, for the shields of the earth belong to God; He is highly exalted.

MEDITATION 2

This psalm is read traditionally on *Rosh HaShanah* (The Feast of Trumpets), New Year's Day on the Jewish calendar. Rosh HaShanah marked the end of the old year and the beginning of the new. It symbolized the creation of the world, as well as the end of the world as we know it. However this is not truly an end, but rather a beginning—portraying the kingship of God as ruler of the eternal kingdom.

This psalm celebrates the enthronement of God over all the earth by looking back at the establishment of Israel in the land (vs. 1–5) and looking forward to the Messianic reign (vs. 6–10), when Yeshua will reign over all the earth "from his throne in Zion." Clapping and shouting were part of the ceremony for enthroning a king (2 Kings 11:12).

> *Then he brought out the king's son, and put the crown upon him, and gave him the testimony, and they proclaimed him king, and anointing him; and they clapped their hands, and said, "Long live the King!"*

In verses one and two the psalmist commands all the peoples of the earth to recognize and join in the crowning of the Lord. The psalmist points out that the Lord is not just one of the local gods of the nations, but "He is king over all the earth." Philippians 2:9–11 says,

> *Therefore God has highly exalted him and bestowed upon him the name which is above every name, that at the name of Yeshua every knee should bow, in heaven and earth, and every tongue confess that Yeshua the Messiah is Lord, to the glory of God the Father.*

Jeremiah 13:11 states in his prophetic word to Israel, God's desire in calling Israel and all people to himself.

> *For as the sash clings to the waist of a man, so I have caused the whole house of Israel and the whole house of Judah to cling to Me,' says the Lord, "that they may become my people,*

for renown, for praise and for glory; but they would not hear.

God's intent was that we should cling to him, and only him, thereby becoming his people. And we, once we becomes his people, are to do these three things:

1. Bring him fame among the nations, to boast of him to our friends and family, to exult in him;
2. To praise him, sing and shout to all who will hear. and sometimes to those who won't hear;
3. To glorify him...proclaim him "King of all the earth."

The last five verses of the sing point to the Messianic reign of Yeshua when all the peoples of the earth gather together in the new Jerusalem to worship the Lord. Revelation 21:22–26 states,

And I saw no temple in the city, for its temple is the Lord God the Almighty and the Lamb. And the city has no need of sun or moon to shine upon it, for the glory of God is its light, and its lamp is the Lamb. By its light shall the nations walk; and the kings of the earth shall bring their glory into it, and its gates shall never be shut by day-and there shall be no night there; they shall bring into it the glory an honor of the nations Revelation 11:15b

...the kingdom of the world has become the kingdom of our Lord and of His Messiah, and He shall reign for ever and ever.

All the shields of earth belong to God. He is greatly exalted!

Dancing Notation
Formation: Circle Dance, HH
Level: Intermediate

PART 1: CHORUS

1. One mayim to left (CW) balance R-L-R-L while facing center
   Repeat #1 three more times

PART 2: VERSES

1. Open mayim to right (CCW) starting with R to the side and L crossing over in front of R, R to the side then L behind R
2. 3-point turn CW (R-L-R) (arms down at sides)
3. Coupé to the right (L-R-L) (L crosses in front of R, stepping on L and clap, R steps in place, L steps to the left side) (hands raised above head on the clap, then lowered to the sides on last 2 counts)
4. Partial coupé to the left (R crosses in the front of L, stepping on R and clap, L steps in place) (hands raised above head on the clap, then lowered to the waist level and join hands on the first balance of #5)
5. Balance R-L-R-L while facing center
   Repeat #5

DANCE TEACHING TIPS

This dance is very high-paced and long. You might find people dropping out occasionally because of exhaustion. Children should always be in the center with their own circle. This is one dance in which accidents can happen. Do not let this stop you from teaching it to your class or congregation, but just take precautions. It is a powerful dance of victory for God's people.

LO AHAVTI DAI
(I Haven't Loved Enough)
Song by Naomi Shemer.
Choreography by Ya'acov (Yankele) Levy
Meditation by Nicole Yoder

Verse 1*

With these hands I haven't built a village.
I haven't found water in the midst of a desert.
I haven't painted a flower,
Or discovered how the road will lead me,
Or whither I go.

Chorus

Aye, I haven't loved enough
The wind and sun on my face,
Aye, I haven't said enough.
And if not now, when?

Verse 2

I haven't sown the grass or built a city.
I haven't planted vineyards on all the hills of chalk.
I haven't done everything with my very own hands
I haven't experienced everything.
I haven't loved enough.

Verse 3

I haven't established a tribe.
I haven't composed a song.
I haven't known snow to fall,
In the middle of the harvest.
I haven't written my memoirs yet
Or built my house of dreams.

*There are no lyrics in the version of *Lo Ahavti Dai* used in *the Messianic Dance International*™ curriculum.

SCRIPTURE SELECTION: ECCLESIATES 12:13, 14

The conclusion, when all has been heard, is: fear God and keep His commandments, because this applies to every person. Because God will bring every act into judgment, everything which is hidden, whether it is good or evil.

MEDITATION

The author of *Lo Ahavti Dai* regrets that he hasn't done many things in life and therefore he concludes that he hasn't loved enough.

One great man in Israel's history, King Solomon, had everything he wanted and still faced the same fundamental question as the author of this song. He wonders what gives meaning to life. Although King Solomon had everything he wanted under the sun, he still found that it was meaningless, pure vanity. His final analysis must be ours as well: What really matters is not what you have or haven't done, but whether you have feared God and kept his commandments.

One day we will stand before God. He will judge each of our acts. The question we must ask ourselves is not, "What have I accomplished?" but "Have I feared God and acknowledged Him in all my ways?"

DANCE NOTATION

Formation: Circle dance, HH.
Level: Beginner

PART 1: VERSES
1. Two mayims to the left (CW), starting with R.
2. Two tcherkessias into the center of the circle. (Hands straight out in front at waist level. palms up when R steps forward, palms down when R steps backward.)
    Repeat #1–2

PART 2: CHORUS

1. Into center, NHH, R-L-R-hop, raising hands to shoulder level, clap on the hop.
2. Backing out, L-R-L-hop, lowering hands to the sides (you can add two claps to the hop).
3. Moving to the right (CCW), do two cross-over leaps (R leaps to the right, L crosses in front, R leaps to the right, L crosses in front) (arms hang down at sides).
4. Three-point turn CW (R-L-R) and L joins R (arms hang down at the sides).

Repeat #1–4

RAM ADONAI
(Great is the Lord)
Song by Naomi Shemer.
Choreography by Ya'acov (Yankele) Levy
Meditation by Nicole Yoder

VERSE 1
Ram Adonai rav lehoshia, rav lehoshia, rav lehoshia
Ram Adonai rav lehoshia, rav lehoshia,
Ha-kaparah hu asa lanu, hu bakhar banu hitzil otanu,
Ram Adonai rav lehoshia, rav lehoshia.

VERSE 2
Ram Adonai noten et Yeshua, noten et Yeshua, noten et Yeshua,
Ram Adonai noten et Yeshua, noten et yeshuato.
Ha-kaparah hu asa lanu, hu bakhar banu hitzil otanu,
Ram Adonai noten et Yeshua, noten et yeshuato.

TRANSLATION
Great is the Lord and mighty to save.
He has made atonement for us.
He has chosen and delivered us.

Great is the Lord who has given us Yeshua.
Great is the Lord who has given us his salvation.
He has made atonement for us.
Great is the Lord who has given us Yeshua,
Given us salvation.

DANCE NOTATION
Formation: Circle dance, facing center, HH.
Level: Beginner

PART 1: VERSES

1. One mayim to the left. Extend R heel to right (2X), arms are at shoulder level, lift with R heel).
2. Back right Yemenite, balance L-R.
3. Close L to R while bending slightly to right, straighten up (face left) while lifting R back (keeping knees together).
4. Repeat #1 & 2.
5. Close L to R.

PART 2: CHORUS

1. Facing CCW, stepping forward. R-L-R-pause...
2. Stepping into center (still facing CCW) L-R-L-pause...
3. On the "pause"—keeping weight on L—pivot 1/4 turn right facing out (release hands, arms in praise mode).
4. Two steps forward R-L.
5. One *rock* back-forward (R-L) (arms cross front and snap back right).
6. Pivot 1/4 turn left (to face CCW) as you repeat #4 & 5.
Repeat #1–6

ENDING

Last time through in Part 2, #6, omit rock forward L and step back L, extend R heel.

INSTRUCTIONAL DANCE PACKAGES
Prepared by *Messianic Dance International*™

Available through LEDERER Publishers and Distributors!

Sets contain instructional video, audio cassette, and study manual. Everything you need to begin!

BEGINNER I: *Embracing Our Jewish Roots*	OO27	$ 39.95
BEGINNER II: *Touching the Hem of His Garment*	OO28	$ 39.95
BEGINNER III: *Keeping it Simple Draws All*	OO21	$ 39.95
ALL 3 INSTRUCTIONAL DANCE PACKAGES	OO29	$109.95

NOTES

CHAPTER 1

[1]J.H. Eaton, cited in Ronald Gagne, Thomas Kane and Robert VerEcke, *Introducing Dance in Christian Worship* (Pastoral Press, 1984), p. 24.

[2]Doug Adams, *Congregation Dancing in Christian Worship* (Sharing Co., 1971), p. 6.

[3]J.G. Davies, *Liturgical Dance: An Historical, Theological and Practical Handbook* (London: SCM Press, 1984), p. 119.

CHAPTER 2

[1]Marilyn Daniels, *The Dance in Christianity* (New York: Paulist Press, 1981), p. 13.

[2]*The Shepherd of Hermas, Parable the Ninth*, (S.9. x). Verse 11, p. 228.

[3]Louis E. Backman, *Religious Dances in the Christian Church and in Popular Medicine* (London: George Allen & Unwin Ltd., 1952), p. 19.

[4]Edgar Hennecke, *New Testament Apocrypha*, Vol. II, ed. by Wilhelm Schneemelcher (Philadelphia:Westminster Press, 1964), p. 229.

[5]Iain H. Murray, citing Gruber, Daniel, *The Church and the Jews: The Biblical Relationship* (Springfield MO: Assemblies of God, 1991), p. 305. In, *The Puritan Hope; Revival and The Interpretation of Prophecy*, (Edinburgh, 1642, 1971), p. 75.

CHAPTER 4

[1]Backman, *Religious Dances*, p. 47.

[2]Carolyn Deitering, *The Liturgy As Dance and the Liturgical Dancer* (New York: Crossroad Pub., 1984), p. 135.

CHAPTER 5
[1]Adams, *Congregational Dancing*, p.2.
[2]Adams, *Congregational Dancing*, p.24.
[3]Davies, *Liturgical Dance*, p. 87.
[4]Daniels, *The Dance*, p. 14.
[5]Backman, *Religious Dances*, p. 27.
[6]H. Schauss, *The Jewish Festivals* (Cincinnati: Union of American Hebrew Congregations, 1938). Cited in Dennis J. Fallon and Mary Jane Wolbers, *Focus On Dance: Religion and Dance*, (Virginia: American Alliance for Health, Physical Education, Recreation and Dance, 1982), p. 41.
[7]*Babylonian Talmud*, Sukkah, 51a–b.

CHAPTER 7
[1]Gagene, et al., *Introducing Dance*, p. 63.
[2]Gagene, et al., *Introducing Dance*, p. 62.
[3]Gagene, et al., *Introducing Dance*, p. 65.